PARTY
Ensembles

This book includes a CD with supplemental content such as
supply lists and patterns. If the CD is missing or damaged,
content can also be found at *www.PaperCraftsMag.com/downloads*

LEISURE
ARTS
the art of everyday living

PAPER CRAFTS

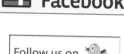

Find us on
Facebook

Follow us on
twitter

www.PaperCraftsMag.com

www.PaperCraftsConnection.com

PARTY Ensembles

Editorial

Editor-in-Chief Jennifer Schaerer
Managing Editor Kerri Miller
Creative Editor Susan R. Opel
Trends Editor Cath Edvalson
Editors Renae Curtz, Courtney Smith
Online Editor P. Kelly Smith
Editorial Assistant Ahtanya Johnson
Contributing Writers Brandy Jesperson, Shelisa Loertscher,
Beth Opel, Nicole Thomas
Copy Editor Susan Hart

Design

Art Director Matt Anderson
Graphic Designer Holly Mills
Photography bpd Studios

Offices

Editorial
Paper Crafts magazine
14850 Pony Express Rd., Suite 200
Bluffdale, UT 84065-4801
Phone 801-816-8300
Fax 801-816-8302
E-mail *editor@PaperCraftsMag.com*
Web site *www.PaperCraftsMag.com*

Published by Leisure Arts, Inc., 5701 Ranch Drive, Little Rock, Arkansas
72223-9633. 501-868-8800. *www.leisurearts.com*

Library of Congress Control Number: 2011938243
ISBN-13/EAN: 978-1-60900-381-4

Leisure Arts Staff

Vice President and Editor-in-Chief Susan White Sullivan
Quilt and Craft Publications Director Cheryl Johnson
Special Projects Director Susan Frantz Wiles
Senior Prepress Director Mark Hawkins
Imaging Technician Stephanie Johnson
Prepress Technician Janie Marie Wright
Publishing Systems Administrator Becky Riddle
Mac Information Technology Specialist Robert Young
President and Chief Executive Officer Rick Barton
Vice President of Sales Mike Behar
Director of Finance and Administration Laticia Mull Dittrich
National Sales Director Martha Adams
Creative Services Chaska Lucus
Information Technology Director Hermine Linz
Controller Frances Caple
Vice President, Operations Jim Dittrich
Retail Customer Service Manager Stan Raynor
Print Production Manager Fred F. Pruss

Creative Crafts Group, LLC

President and CEO: Stephen J. Kent
VP/Group Publisher: Tina Battock
Chief Financial Officer: Mark F. Arnett
Controller: Jordan Bohrer
VP/Publishing Director: Joel P. Toner
VP/Production & Technology: Barbara Schmitz
VP/Circulation: Nicole McGuire

Visit our web sites:
www.PaperCraftsMag.com
www.PaperCraftsConnection.com
www.MoxieFabWorld.com

PUBLICATION—*Paper Crafts*™ (ISSN 1548-5706) (USPS 506250), is published 6 times per year in Jan/Feb, Mar/Apr, May/June, Jul/Aug, Sept/Oct and Nov/Dec, by Creative Crafts Group, LLC, 741 Corporate Circle, Suite A, Golden CO 80401. Periodicals postage paid at Salt Lake City, UT and additional mailing offices.

REPRINT PERMISSION—For information on obtaining reprints and excerpts, please contact Wright's Reprints at 877/652-5295. (Customers outside the U.S. and Canada should call 281/419-5725.)

TRADEMARKED NAMES mentioned in this book may not always be followed with a trademark symbol. The names are used only in an editorial fashion and to the benefit of the trademark owner, with no intention of infringement of the trademark.

PROJECTS—*Paper Crafts* magazine believes these projects are reliable when made, but none are guaranteed. Due to different climatic conditions and variations in materials, *Paper Crafts* disclaims any liability for untoward results in doing the projects represented. Use of the publication does not guarantee successful results. We provide this information WITHOUT WARRANTY OF ANY KIND, EXPRESSED, IMPLIED, OR STATUTORY; AND WE SPECIFICALLY DISCLAIM ANY IMPLIED WARRANTIES OF MERCHANTABILITY OR FITNESS FOR A PARTICULAR PURPOSE. Also, we urge parents to supervise young children carefully in their participation in any of these projects.

Posted under Canadian Publication Agreement Number 0551724

Make it a Party!

From the times of your life such as birthdays, anniversaries, baby showers, and religious celebrations to holidays and seasonal occasions, there's no better way to add your own personal touch to the festivities than with a paper-crafted party ensemble. Make cute picks for plain cupcakes, set out personalized place cards, or wrap a napkin in a clever ring of paper, and you've got the beginnings of a time to remember.

Don't stop there though. Simple everyday events can become fun and festive special occasions when you add a paper-crafted theme – book club, movie night, wine tasting, a crafty gathering of girlfriends, and even a family dinner will turn into instant celebrations with the inspiration you'll find in these pages. I decided to put a party spin on a regular family meal in our house with a Swiss-themed cheese fondue ensemble (see below). It sure would be fun to use bright neon hues too, and invite friends to join us for a disco-themed fondue party. Let your creativity flow, because the possibilities are endless when you consider changing a color scheme or using a different pattern.

Everything you need is included in these pages or on the CD inside the back cover (where you'll find full supply lists, patterns, and digital design elements). Go ahead and make your next gathering extra special by whipping up some paper-crafted fun!

Jennifer

Find instructions for this **SWISS FONDUE** Ensemble on *p. 288.*

PARTY Ensembles

Contents

p. 165

p. 41

p. 129

p. 17

p. 91

PAPER CRAFTS
MAGAZINE®

www.PaperCraftsMag.com
www.PaperCraftsConnection.com

Love to Shop

Designer: Alicia Thelin

(a) INVITATION

1. Make card from cardstock.
2. Border-punch patterned paper strip; adhere inside card front.
3. Cut patterned paper strip, adhere around card, and adhere ribbon. Slot-punch end and tie on ribbon.
4. Apply bar code rub-on.
5. Stamp large rose, small rose, and 100% label on cardstock; trim. Stitch label and apply you're invited rub-on to large rose. Adhere to card with foam tape.

(b) PURSE FAVOR

1. Emboss cardstock; die-cut into two baskets. Trim into purse shape.
2. Cut cardstock strip, fold, and adhere between die cuts.
3. Cut pocket from patterned paper; adhere with foam tape.
4. Fill with candy and tie on ribbon.

(c) PLACE CARD

1. Cut cardstock to 4¼" x 11¼". Fold at 2", 5", 8", and 10" to form triangle. Round top corners and adhere flaps.
2. Border-punch edge of cardstock strip. Apply shopping sentiment rub-on and adhere three sides to form pocket.
3. Stamp name on cardstock. Punch into tags, string on twine, and tie on card. Adhere tags with foam tape.
4. Insert gift card.

(d) PIGGY BANK

1. Stamp check list on cardstock, trim into tag, and round right corners.
2. Border-punch cardstock piece and adhere behind tag. Attach brad.
3. Tie ribbon around piggy bank. Tie tag to ribbon with crochet thread.

(e) BANNER

1. Fold patterned paper strips. Die-cut pennants from strips, leaving fold intact.
2. Stamp "Party" across pennants.
3. Punch flowers and circles from cardstock, layer, and adhere to unstamped pennants.
4. Thread pennants on twine. Adhere pennants together.

(f) GIFT BAG

1. Cut patterned paper to fit gift bag; adhere patterned paper strip. Stitch edges and adhere to bag.
2. Die-cut rosette from patterned paper; assemble.
3. Stamp sentiment on cardstock, punch into circle, and adhere to rosette.
4. Emboss patterned paper strip; sand and notch end. Cut patterned paper strip, notch end, and adhere to embossed strip. Adhere twine. Adhere to embossed strip bag and adhere rosette.

(g) THANK YOU CARD

1. Make card from cardstock; round top corners.
2. Adhere patterned paper strip. Cut patterned paper strip, pleat, and zigzag-stitch. Punch half-circle from one end, tie on twine, and adhere to card.
3. Cut patterned paper strip, stamp much appreciated, and stitch. Adhere with foam tape.
4. Stamp small rose on cardstock, trim, and adhere with foam tape. Adhere epoxy flower.

Try this

Give each party guest a gift card, tucked into her place card, and some cash for lunch at the shopping center.

Crossword Birthday

Designer: Alicia Thelin

ⓐ INVITATION

1. Make card from cardstock; round top corners.
2. Punch half-circle from left edge of card front. Punch circle from cardstock and fold over card edge. Punch hole and tie on twine.
3. Adhere cardstock strip. Border-punch strip of wood paper, adhere, and staple.
4. Stamp Crossword Background on cardstock, cut into circle using template, and adhere with foam tape.
5. Stamp sentiment arrow on cardstock, trim, and adhere with foam tape.

ⓑ CARD

1. Make card from cardstock; trim card front into curve using template.
2. Adhere cardstock inside card.
3. Cut wood paper strip, border-punch, and adhere. Tie on twine.
4. Stamp Crossword Background on cardstock and cut into circle using template. Stamp happy birthday, attach brad, and adhere with foam tape.
5. Punch arrow from cardstock and adhere with foam tape. Attach paperclip.

ⓒ CHAIN

1. Stamp Crossword Background on both sides of cardstock.
2. Cut 36 strips at 2½" x ½". Staple ends of each strip, looping each through the last before stapling.
3. Tie on twine at chain ends.

ⓓ TREAT BOX

1. Die-cut two milk cartons from cardstock. Stamp to open on each and assemble.
2. Attach clothespins.
3. Make box, following pattern found on included CD.
4. Cut cardstock strip; adhere around box. Tie on ribbon. Place milk cartons in box.
5. Stamp Crossword Background on wood paper; punch into circle. Stamp got treats?, punch hole, and attach to ribbon with jump ring.

ⓔ BOTTLE WRAP

1. Cut wood paper strips; border-punch one short end. Punch hole.
2. Wrap strips around bottles, thread with twine and tie.
3. Stamp Crossword Background on cardstock; punch into circles. Stamp got birthday?, punch hole, and attach to twine with jump rings.

Try this

Make a personalized crossword puzzle for a party game. Use facts about the birthday celebrant and give out prizes!

ⓐ

ⓔ

ⓒ

ⓑ

ⓓ

GOT BIRTHDAY?

GOT BIRTHDAY?

PaRty
THIS WAY

happy birthday

TO OPEN

TO OPEN

GOT TREATS?

Young Pilot Birthday

Designer: Rebecca Oehlers

ⓐ BANNER

1. Die-cut large banner flags from cardstock. Die-cut medium banner flags from patterned paper.
2. Adhere medium flags to large flags; zigzag-stitch edges.
3. Punch scalloped circles from cardstock and stamp "Birthday boy" on circles. Mat with scalloped circles punched from cardstock.
4. Cut cardstock strips, stamp polka dots, and border-punch one edge.
5. Adhere scalloped circles and strips to flags with foam tape. Adhere buttons.
6. Stamp planes on cardstock; color and trim. Die-cut large and small clouds from cardstock; detail with marker. Adhere to flags with foam tape. Hang flags on twine.

ⓑ GOODIE BAG

1. Cut patterned paper panel; mat with cardstock. Border-punch cardstock strip and adhere behind panel. Adhere panel to bag.
2. Cut patterned paper strip, accordion-fold, and adhere.
3. Stamp plane, banner, and hey buddy! on cardstock; color and trim.
4. Die-cut large and small clouds from cardstock; detail with marker. Adhere large cloud to bag. Adhere other images with foam tape.

ⓒ PLACEMAT

1. Cut cardstock to finished size.
2. Adhere patterned paper piece and strip; zigzag-stitch seam.
3. Border-punch edge of patterned paper strip; adhere.
4. Die-cut large and small clouds from cardstock; detail with marker and adhere.
5. Stamp plane, banner, and happy birthday! on cardstock; color, trim, and adhere.

ⓓ PLACE CARD

1. Make card from cardstock.
2. Cut cardstock panel, adhere ends of twine behind panel, and adhere to card.
3. Cut cardstock strip, mat with cardstock, notch ends, and adhere. Adhere buttons.
4. Stamp plane on cardstock; color, trim, and adhere.
5. Die-cut large clouds from cardstock; detail with marker. Stamp guest's name on clouds, color, and adhere with foam tape. Attach clothespins.

Try this

Make up little passports for your young pilots! Have them "fly" to different countries and experience the culture. Use chopsticks in China, origami in Japan, or try some Gummi Bears in Germany!

Spy Birthday

Designer: Betsy Veldman

(a) INVITATION

1. Die-cut file folder from patterned paper.
2. Adhere vellum inside window. Stitch sides closed to form pocket.
3. Print "Secret decoder" on cardstock; trim, ink edges, and adhere.
4. Stamp sentiment label; trim, ink edges, and adhere. Stamp dotted circle on patterned paper, punch into circle, add fingerprint, and adhere. Attach paperclip.
5. Print party details on cardstock. *Note: Use light blue ink.* Stamp background over words, using Pure Poppy ink. Trim to fit inside pocket, round top corners, and ink edges.
6. Adhere strip of patterned paper to insert. Stamp original circle and sentiment label.

(b) BOOK

1. Cover front and back of book with patterned paper.
2. Die-cut confidential from cardstock; adhere.
3. Stamp original circle and sentiment label. Add fingerprint.

(c) CAMERA WRAP

1. Cut patterned paper strip; wrap around camera and adhere ends.
2. Print camera circle on cardstock; cut out and punch hole. Thread with twine and tie on camera.
3. Die-cut classified from cardstock; mat with patterned paper and adhere.

(d) FAVOR BOX

1. Cover recipe box with patterned paper; sand and ink edges.
2. Print crime scene circle on cardstock, trim, and adhere.
3. Stamp original circle and sentiment label.
4. Die-cut classified and confidential from cardstock; adhere.

(e) GLASSES TAG

1. Trim patterned paper into tag; ink edges. Attach eyelet.
2. Die-cut shhh from cardstock; adhere.
3. Tie tag to glasses with twine.

(f) FOOD PICK

1. Die-cut scalloped circles from patterned paper.
2. Stamp circle borders on patterned paper and punch into circles. Add fingerprint.
3. Adhere circles and scalloped circles with skewer between.

(g) BOTTLE WRAP

1. Cut patterned paper panel; adhere to bottle.
2. Print "Top secret recipe" on patterned paper; trim into strip.
3. Stamp original circle and sentiment label on printed strip and adhere.
4. Adhere patterned paper strips.
5. Stamp original circle on patterned paper, punch into circle, and adhere to bottle cap.

(h) MOUSTACHES

1. Download moustache patterns found on CD. Print on cardstock and trim.
2. Adhere to dowels.

Designer Tip

"Top secret recipe" and "secret decoder" sentiments can be found on the attached CD.

Try this

Have party guests dress in their best under-cover spy disguises, fingerprint each guest as they come in the door, and then lead the guests on a secret mission to find their goody bags.

Fun on the Farm

Designer: Chan Vuong

(a) INVITATION

1. Make card from cardstock; cover with patterned paper.
2. Die-cut and emboss small label from cardstock; adhere with foam tape.
3. Adhere felt sheep.
4. Print "Ewe are invited" on cardstock, trim, and adhere with foam tape.

(b) THANK YOU CARD

1. Make card from cardstock; cover with patterned paper.
2. Die-cut and emboss small label from cardstock; adhere with foam tape.
3. Adhere felt cow.
4. Print "Thank moo" on cardstock, trim, and adhere with foam tape.

(c) PLACEMAT

1. Die-cut large label from patterned paper.
2. Die-cut medium label from patterned paper; adhere.
3. Affix flowers sticker.

(d) PLACE CARD

1. Make card from cardstock.
2. Adhere journaling card. Adhere felt barn.
3. Write guest name with marker.

(e) NAPKIN RING

1. Cut patterned paper strip; adhere ends to form ring.
2. Adhere tomato sticker to cardstock; trim. Adhere to ring with foam tape.

(f) COASTER

1. Die-cut and emboss scalloped circle from coaster.
2. Stamp polka dots.
3. Affix peas sticker.

See detailed image of coaster on p. 287.

(g) FAVOR BAG

1. Fold top of bag to form flap. Cut patterned paper to fit bag front and flap, round corners, and adhere.
2. Die-cut rosette from patterned paper; assemble.
3. Die-cut and emboss small starburst circle from patterned paper; adhere to rosette. Adhere felt pear.
4. Cut patterned paper strips, notch ends, and adhere to flap. Adhere rosette.

(h) FAVOR BOX

1. Cut patterned paper strip and adhere around pillow box.
2. Wrap with twine and tie.
3. Die-cut circle and medium starburst circle from patterned paper; layer and adhere together.
4. Adhere felt apple. Adhere piece to pillow box with foam tape.

(i) CUPCAKE TOPPER

1. Die-cut rosette from patterned paper; assemble.
2. Die-cut and emboss small starburst circle from patterned paper; adhere to rosette.
3. Adhere desired felt accent. Adhere rosette to lollipop stick.

Try this

This ensemble can also work well as a summer party complete with farm fresh corn, watermelon and tomatoes.

Space Monkey Birthday

Designer: Chan Vuong

(a) INVITATION

1. Make card from cardstock; round right corners.
2. Trim alien circle die cut; adhere.
3. Stamp you're invited on cardstock, trim into speech bubble, and adhere with foam tape.

(b) PLACEMAT

1. Die-cut large label from cardstock.
2. Die-cut medium label from cardstock; adhere.
3. Affix rocket, star, and comet stickers.

(c) PLACE CARD

1. Make card from cardstock.
2. Adhere patterned paper to cardstock; trim and adhere to card.
3. Affix small star sticker. Adhere alien and star stickers with foam tape.
4. Write guest name with marker.

(d) COASTER

1. Stamp polka dots on coaster.
2. Die-cut and emboss starburst circle from cardstock; adhere.
3. Circle-punch space monkey from patterned paper; adhere.

(e) CAN WRAP

1. Cut cardstock strip with decorative-edge scissors; wrap around can and adhere ends.
2. Die-cut and emboss starburst circle from cardstock.
3. Circle-punch space monkey from patterned paper, adhere to circle, and adhere to can with foam tape.

(f) TREAT BAG TOPPER

1. Die-cut curved rectangles from patterned paper and cardstock. Adhere together and fold.
2. Adhere monkey sticker with foam tape.
3. Adhere over resealable bag.

(g) CUPCAKE TOPPERS

1. Affix alien, planet, star, stitched star, starburst, and U.F.O. stickers to cardstock; trim.
2. Adhere starburst, planet, and stitched star to lollipop sticks.
3. Adhere remaining stickers with foam tape.

Try this

Attach little paper flags to toothpicks and use them on a Swiss cheese "moon".

Turning Three

Designer: Davinie Fiero

ⓐ INVITATION

1. Make card from cardstock.
2. Cut patterned paper panel; border-punch bottom edge.
3. Adhere patterned paper strips; stitch. Adhere to card.
4. Affix stickers to spell "You're invited".
5. Punch stars from patterned paper and adhere, using foam tape for one. Adhere button.

ⓑ GARLAND

1. Punch circles and stars from patterned paper.
2. Stitch pieces together.

ⓒ PARTY HAT

1. Cut hat from patterned paper, following pattern found on CD. Adhere.
2. Cut "3" from patterned paper; mat with cardstock, trim, and adhere with foam tape.
3. Cut patterned paper strip, pleat, and adhere.
4. Punch stars from patterned paper; adhere. Adhere buttons.

ⓓ PARTY BAG

1. Punch circle from patterned paper. Mat with scalloped circle punched from patterned paper; adhere.
2. Punch star from patterned paper; adhere.
3. Punch holes in bag, thread with twine, string on button, and tie bow.

ⓔ CUPCAKE PICK

1. Punch scalloped circles from patterned paper.
2. Punch stars from patterned paper; adhere buttons.
3. Adhere toothpicks between stars and scalloped circles.

ⓕ BUBBLE WRAP

1. Cut patterned paper strip; adhere around bubbles.
2. Punch star from patterned paper; adhere.

Try this

Have three balloons attached to the bubbles for each guest to take home at the end of the party.

Sweet 16

Designer: Joannie McBride

ⓐ CARD

1. Make card from patterned paper. Adhere patterned paper panel.
2. Spray doily with ink; let dry. Punch circles and scalloped circles from patterned paper. Adhere doily and punched pieces, using foam tape between layers.
3. Affix sentiment and embellished circle stickers.
4. Adhere rhinestone. Tie on ribbon. Knot ribbon on pin; attach.

ⓑ FRAME

1. Spray doily with ink; let dry. Adhere.
2. Affix polka dot banner, cake, oh, happy, day, and floral circle stickers.
3. Tie ribbon bow; adhere. Adhere one circle and six circle stickers with foam tape.
4. Knot ribbon on pin; attach.

ⓒ BOTTLES

1. Spray doilies with ink; let dry. Adhere to bottles.
2. Punch circles and scalloped circles from patterned paper; layer and adhere. Adhere rhinestones.
3. Affix laugh, celebrate, and eat cake stickers to tags. Tie tags to bottles with ribbon and tulle.
4. Attach pin to one bottle.

ⓓ CONE

1. Trim circle from patterned paper, cut slit to center, and roll to form cone; staple.
2. Punch holes and thread with ribbon to form handle. Adhere ribbon around cone.
3. Spray doilies with ink; let dry. Fold in half and adhere to cone. Tie on ribbon and attach pin.
4. Punch circle and scalloped circles from patterned paper; layer and adhere with foam tape. Adhere rhinestone.

ⓔ CUPCAKE STANDS

1. Assemble stands. Spray with ink and let dry.
2. Cut apart party banner sticker and affix to stands.
3. Adhere rhinestones and tie on ribbon.

ⓕ CUPCAKE PICK

1. Punch circles from patterned paper and adhere with lollipop stick between.
2. Punch circles and scalloped circles from patterned paper; layer and adhere.
3. Adhere rhinestone.

Try this

Crumple the punched circles and scalloped circles slightly for added texture and dimension.

Grandma's 70th Birthday

Designer: Julia Stainton

ⓐ INVITATION

1. Make card from cardstock; ink edges.
2. Cut patterned paper panel, mat with patterned paper, and adhere.
3. Print sentiment on cardstock; trim, ink, and distress edges. Affix number stickers. Fold ticket in half and attach with staples. Adhere piece to card.
4. Tie on twine. Tie seam binding bow and adhere. Adhere flower and attach leaf pin.

ⓑ PENDANT

1. Cut cardstock to fit in metal frame; cover with patterned paper. Insert glass and piece in frame.
2. Apply rub-ons to glass.
3. Adhere resin frame and affix monogram sticker.
4. Attach crown and charm to pendant with jump ring.
5. String pendant on seam binding.

See detailed image of pendant on p. 287

ⓒ GUEST BOOK

1. Cover album front and inside pages with patterned paper; sand cover edges.
2. Adhere doily. Tie seam binding bow and adhere.
3. Adhere flower die cuts, using foam tape as desired.
4. Attach pearl pins.
5. Affix stickers to spell "Guests".

ⓓ FRAME

1. Cover frame with patterned paper strips; sand edges.
2. Adhere lace.
3. Tear strip of canvas, roll into flower, and adhere. Adhere to frame.
4. Adhere rhinestone and leaves.

ⓔ FOOD PICK

1. Thread canvas flag on toothpick.
2. Punch flower from patterned paper; adhere.
3. Adhere rhinestone.

ⓕ PLACE CARD

1. Make card from cardstock.
2. Adhere acrylic doily. Tie seam binding bow and adhere.
3. Spray flower with ink; let dry and adhere.
4. Affix stickers to spell guest name.

ⓖ SHADOW BOX

1. Cut photos and patterned paper panels to fit inside shadow box sections.
2. Stamp love sentiment on one patterned paper panel; adhere photos and panels. Affix tape sticker around box.
3. Create word strips with label maker; affix.
4. Adhere filmstrip die cut, heart pin, flower, and sequin button.
5. Thread canvas flag with seam binding, tie bow, and adhere. Affix monogram sticker.

Try this

For milestone birthdays, put together a slideshow presentation of the guest of honor's life. Change the guest book into a memory album by including photos from the special event.

when
i want
to see love
defined i
look at you

WIFE   MOM
SISTER
GRANDMA
FRIEND

guests

Someone special
is turning...

70

Come celebrate
with us!

Garden Party Birthday

Designer: Julia Stainton

ⓐ INVITATION

1. Make card from cardstock; ink edges.
2. Cut patterned paper panel, ink and distress edges, and adhere.
3. Print sentiment on adhesive-back canvas. Stamp flowers, trim, and affix.
4. Adhere leaf. Affix bird and epoxy dot stickers.
5. Adhere twigs and tie on twine.

ⓑ BIRD HOUSE

1. Cover birdhouse with patterned paper; sand edges.
2. Tie on tulle.
3. Adhere flowers and leaf pins.
4. Place moss inside birdhouse. Affix butterfly sticker.

ⓒ GIFT BOXES

1. Die-cut pillow boxes from patterned paper; assemble.
2. Tie on twine.
3. Adhere leaf, flower, and butterfly stickers.

ⓓ NAPKIN

1. Tear canvas fabric into square.
2. Stamp butterfly in one corner; heat-set.

ⓔ NAPKIN RING

1. Cut strip of transparency sheet; staple into ring.
2. Punch circle from cardstock; ink edges.
3. Affix dragonfly and epoxy dot stickers to circle. Adhere circle to ring.

ⓕ PLACE CARD

1. Make card from cardstock.
2. Paint chipboard frame; let dry.
3. Cut patterned paper to fit behind frame; adhere.
4. Affix stickers to spell guest names.
5. Tie twine bow; adhere.

Designer Tip

Reduce waste when using adhesive-back canvas sheets by printing an entire sheet of sentiments at once, rather than just the one you need right now.

Try this

Accent your table with tea lights in mason jars and little pots of flowers or fresh herbs.

Remember the Good Old Days

Designer: Kalyn Kepner

(a) INVITATION

1. Make card from cardstock.
2. Stamp music and you're invited.
3. Stitch card edges.
4. Layer and affix tile and border or other stickers, using foam tape as desired.
5. Thread button with floss and adhere.

(b) BANNER

1. Cut triangles from patterned paper; mat with cardstock.
2. Trim cardstock strips with decorative-edge scissors; adhere.
3. Adhere lace to top of every other triangle. Trim patterned paper strips with decorative-edge scissors and adhere to remaining triangles.
4. Die-cut scalloped circles from cardstock; ink edges.
5. Print "Party" on cardstock; trim letters into circles. Ink edges and mat with scalloped circles. Adhere to triangles with foam tape.
6. Thread buttons with floss and adhere. Adhere triangles to ribbon to form banner.

(c) GIFT BOX

1. Cut patterned paper strips; adhere around box.
2. Adhere lace.
3. Affix pears label and fresh eggs sticker.

(d) PLACE CARD

1. Make card from cardstock; ink edges.
2. Adhere patterned paper strip.
3. Print guest name on cardstock; trim. Stamp music.
4. Mat name piece with cardstock, trim with decorative-edge scissors and adhere.
5. Thread buttons with floss; adhere.

(e) CUPCAKE TOPPER

1. Die-cut scalloped circle from patterned paper; stitch border.
2. Thread buttons with floss; adhere.
3. Print "1¢" on cardstock; trim into circle and ink edges.
4. Mat circle with patterned paper, trim with decorative-edge scissors, and adhere with foam tape.
5. Adhere to toothpick.

(f) CANDY JAR WRAP

1. Die-cut and emboss label from cardstock. Stitch edges.
2. Punch holes in label sides and thread with ribbon.
3. Die-cut scalloped circle from patterned paper and adhere with foam tape.
4. Print sentiment on cardstock, cut into circle, and ink edges. Stitch edges and adhere with foam tape.
5. Thread buttons with floss and adhere.

(g) SODA WRAP

1. Cut wrap from cardstock. Trim patterned paper strips with decorative-edge scissors and adhere.
2. Trim patterned paper, adhere, and stitch edges.
3. Print sentiment on cardstock, cut into circle, and ink edges.
4. Notch ends of patterned paper strip, adhere behind printed circle, and adhere to wrap with foam tape.

(h) FRAME

1. Cover frame with patterned paper and ink edges.
2. Trim patterned paper strips with decorative-edge scissors; adhere.
3. Fussy-cut flowers from patterned paper; adhere.
4. Affix photo corners, windmill, jar, flower circle, and date tile stickers.

Designer Tip

Titles for the candy and soda wraps can be found on the included CD.

Try This

Activities in keeping with a vintage theme could include Bingo and taking photo-booth-style pictures.

Our Little Lion is One

Designer: Katie Stilwater

(a) INVITATION

1. Make card from cardstock.
2. Print party details on cardstock; trim. Adhere to card.
3. Die-cut lion from cardstock; adhere to card.
4. Punch circles from patterned paper and adhere.

(b) CUPCAKE TOPPER

1. Die-cut lion from cardstock and patterned paper. Die-cut hat and asterisk from cardstock.
2. Adhere together and adhere to toothpick.

(c) CUPCAKE WRAPPER

1. Die-cut wrapper from cardstock; assemble.
2. Die-cut "1" and scalloped circle from cardstock; adhere together.
3. Adhere circle to wrapper with foam tape.

(d) CUPCAKE STAND

1. Paint candle stick and disc; let dry.
2. Adhere disc to candle stick.
3. Punch circles from patterned paper; adhere.

(e) FAVOR BAG

1. Die-cut basket from patterned paper; assemble.
2. Stamp circle frame, lion, and party animal on cardstock; color. Punch into circle.
3. Mat stamped circle with scalloped circle punched from cardstock. Adhere with foam tape.

(f) BANNER

1. Die-cut pennants, lions, and "Roar!" from cardstock.
2. Cut cardstock strips, border-punch, and adhere to pennants.
3. Adhere letters and lions to pennants.
4. Punch circles from patterned paper. Punch holes in pennants and circles; string on twine to form banner.

(g) PARTY HAT

1. Print party hat template found on CD on cardstock; trim and assemble.
2. Die-cut lion from cardstock and patterned paper. Die-cut "1" from cardstock.
3. Punch scalloped circle from cardstock. Adhere "1", adhere lion with foam tape, and adhere piece to hat with foam tape.
4. Punch circles from patterned paper; adhere around hat.
5. Cut asterisk from cardstock and adhere.

(h) MOBILE

1. Paint embroidery hoop; let dry.
2. Punch circles from patterned paper. Die-cut lions and numbers from cardstock; punch holes in tops.
3. Stitch strips of circles.
4. Tie numbers and lions to ends of circle strips.
5. Tie strips to embroidery hoop.

(i) THANK YOU CARD

1. Make card from cardstock.
2. Emboss cardstock panel; adhere.
3. Punch circles from patterned paper; adhere.
4. Stamp circle frame, thanks, and lion on cardstock; color and punch into circle.
5. Mat stamped circle with scalloped circle punched from cardstock. Adhere with foam tape.

Designer Tip

The text for the invite can be found on the included CD.

Try This

Create a larger-scale lion and play "Pin the tail on the lion".

ROAR!

You're invited for some fun,
Our Little Lion is turning one!

Please join us for a
ROARing good time!

March 2nd
3:00 p.m.
Our House

THANKS

party animal

Surfer Dude Birthday

Designer: Kim Hughes

(a) INVITATION

1. Print party details on patterned paper; trim.
2. Cut surfboard from patterned paper, following pattern found on CD.
3. Adhere patterned paper piece and brad topper punched from patterned paper; trim.
4. Adhere surfboard. Tie on twine.

(b) PLACEMAT

1. Cut overlapped surfboards from patterned paper, following pattern.
2. Adhere patterned paper strip.
3. Punch brad topper from patterned paper; adhere.

(c) PLACE CARD

1. Make card from patterned paper. Adhere patterned paper strips.
2. Cut surfboard, following pattern. Adhere.
3. Affix stickers to spell guest's name.

(d) BOTTLE CARRIER

1. Cut patterned paper to fit front panel of carrier; adhere. Adhere patterned paper strips.
2. Cut surfboard from patterned paper, following pattern. Adhere patterned paper strip and adhere to carrier.

(e) BOTTLE WRAP

1. Cut patterned paper strip; adhere around bottle neck. Tie on twine.
2. Cut patterned paper strip, adhere patterned paper pieces, and adhere around bottle.

(f) FOOD PICK

1. Cut mini surfboards from patterned paper, following pattern found on CD.
2. Adhere patterned paper strips or punches.
3. Adhere to toothpicks.

(g) CONTEST TAG

1. Cut tag from patterned paper; adhere patterned paper strip.
2. Print contest details on patterned paper; trim and adhere.
3. Adhere patterned paper strip. Punch brad topper from patterned paper; trim and adhere.
4. Punch hole and tie on twine.

(h) BANNER

1. Cut triangles from patterned paper. Adhere patterned paper piece to one.
2. Punch brad toppers from patterned paper; adhere.
3. Affix stickers on triangles to spell "Dude".
4. Punch holes in triangles and thread on twine to form banner.

Designer Tip

The invitation and surf contest sentiments can be found on the included CD.

Try This

Bring in some sand to add around the party table or grind up some graham crackers for an edible version. Use blue punch or blue raspberry soda for a drink that looks like the ocean.

Surf Contest

Stall	score_____
Rodeo Flip	score_____
A-Frame	score_____
Ace Tone	score_____
Re-entry	score_____

Aloha
Betty or Bro,

DUDE!

Come to my totally awesome
beach party

Saturday, July 2, 2011
From low tide to high tide

Bring your board!

STAY-N-PLAY

ED

D U D E

Back to the '80s Bash

Designer: Kim Kesti

ⓐ INVITATION

1. Make card from cardstock. Adhere cardstock panel.
2. Print sentiment on cardstock; trim and adhere.
3. Adhere cardstock strip and affix stickers to spell "Dude".
4. Cut game figures from cardstock using the pattern found on included CD; adhere. Punch eyes from cardstock; adhere.
5. Punch circle from cardstock, trim mouth, and adhere. Punch circles from cardstock; adhere.

ⓑ POSTER

1. Trim cardstock.
2. Punch circles from cardstock and patterned paper; adhere.
3. Affix stickers to spell sentiment. *Note: Leave space for heart.*
4. Cut heart from cardstock, apply glitter, and adhere to poster with foam tape.

ⓒ CD CASE

1. Print playlist on cardstock; trim to fit inside case front.
2. Adhere patterned paper and cardstock strips.
3. Affix stickers to spell "Rock on".
4. Insert piece inside case.

ⓓ CAMERA PLACARD

1. Cut cardstock to 7" x 6"; score at 1" and 6", fold, and cut down to create tabs.
2. Adhere cardstock strips.
3. Print sentiment on cardstock; trim and adhere.
4. Affix stickers to spell "Gnarly".
5. Adhere camera to placard.

ⓔ GIFT CARD HOLDER

1. Make card from cardstock.
2. Adhere cardstock piece and strip.
3. Cut patterned paper and adhere on three sides to form pocket.
4. Print sentiment on cardstock; punch into circle. Double-mat with circles punched from cardstock; adhere to card.
5. Affix stickers to spell "4 You".

ⓕ NAPKIN RING

1. Trim cardstock strip.
2. Adhere cardstock strips and ribbon.
3. Adhere ends to form ring; attach brad.

Designer Tip

Create your own playlist of your favorite '80s songs for the CD party favor.

Try This

Have your guests dress in iconic '80s wear: big hair, glitter eye shadow, lots of neon, leg warmers, and side ponytails, etc.

ⓔ 4 YOU — like totally have a great birthday

ⓑ I ♥ 80'S

snap photos that are totally GNARLY

Kodak

ⓓ

ⓕ

ⓒ

Another One Bites the Dust – Queen
Celebration – Kool & The Gang
Whip It! – Devo
I Love Rock and Roll – Joan Jett & the Blackhearts
Rock the Casbah – Clash
Beat It – Michael Jackson
Born in the USA – Bruce Springsteen
The Power of Love – Huey Lewis & The News
What's Love Got To Do With It – Tina Turner
Time after Time – Cyndi Lauper
Start Me Up – Rolling Stones

ROCK ON

ⓐ DUDE A totally radical 80's party

Birthday in Blue

Designer: Latisha Yoast

ⓐ CUPCAKE TOPPERS

1. Die-cut and emboss large leaves from patterned paper; adhere together over toothpicks.
2. Die-cut and emboss leaves from patterned paper; adhere with foam tape.
3. Adhere sticker with foam tape.

ⓑ PLACE CARD

1. Die-cut and emboss two leaves from patterned paper; adhere together at top to form card.
2. Die-cut and emboss leaf from patterned paper. Stamp guest name and adhere to card with foam tape.
3. Affix leaf stem sticker with foam tape.

ⓒ FAVOR BAG

1. Trim patterned paper panel, stamp thank you, and adhere to bag.
2. Die-cut and emboss label from patterned paper; trim and adhere.
3. Adhere flower sticker with foam tape.

ⓓ POPCORN CONTAINER

1. Make container, following pattern found on CD.
2. Die-cut and emboss leaf from patterned paper; adhere with foam tape.
3. Adhere flower sticker with foam tape.
4. Tie on twine.

ⓔ GIFT BAG

1. Affix border sticker to gift bag.
2. Stamp wishing you and sentiment.
3. Die-cut and emboss circle from patterned paper; trim and adhere.
4. Adhere bird sticker with foam tape.
5. Tie on twine.

ⓕ PARTY HAT

1. Cut patterned paper in circle, slit to center, and roll to form hat; adhere.
2. Roll patterned paper, cut slits in one end, and adhere in top of hat. Curl strips.
3. Staple twill.
4. Die-cut and emboss leaves from cardstock and patterned paper. Stamp happy on patterned paper leaf, adhere to cardstock leaf with foam tape, and adhere to hat with foam tape.

ⓖ BANNER

1. Die-cut pennants and lacy pennants from patterned paper. Adhere together using foam tape.
2. Die-cut and emboss leaves from patterned paper.
3. Stamp "Party" on leaves, color, and adhere to pennants with foam tape.
4. Punch tops of pennants and thread on twill to form banner.
5. Tie on ribbon at ends.

Try This

Ask everyone to wear blue to the party and then snap a picture of the group for a fun memento.

Gnome Birthday

Designer: Laura O'Donnell

ⓐ BOOK FAVOR

1. Cover front and back of book with patterned paper; finish with decoupage.
2. Open desired image in software, resize as desired, and print on photo paper.
3. Trim image and adhere. Seal with another coat of decoupage.

ⓑ INVITATION MAGNET

1. Cut tag from cardstock; round corners.
2. Print party details on patterned paper; trim, round corners, and distress edges. Adhere to tag.
3. Open gnome in software, resize as desired, and print on photo paper. Trim and adhere.
4. Open banner in software; resize to 3½" wide. Type "Save the date", warp text 15 degrees to fit banner, and print on photo paper. Trim and adhere to tag with foam tape.
5. Adhere piece of magnet behind tag.
6. Print heart on photo paper, trim, and adhere to envelope flap.

ⓒ CUPCAKE TOPPERS

1. Punch large circles from cardstock; adhere together with toothpicks between.
2. Punch medium circles from patterned paper, distress edges, and adhere.
3. Open mushrooms and heart in software, resize as desired, and print on photo paper.
4. Trim images. Adhere mushrooms with foam tape.
5. Mat heart with cardstock, cut second cardstock heart, and adhere together with toothpick between.

ⓓ GIFT BAG

1. Cut patterned paper, distress edges, and adhere to gift bag.
2. Open gnome, mushrooms, and heart in software. Resize as desired and print on photo paper.
3. Trim images and adhere, using foam tape for gnome.
4. Punch hole in heart and tie on with twine.

Designer Tip

Local companies often use magnets as advertisements in the mail, or attached to a new phone book. These make great sheet magnets in your crafting projects!

save the date

Uncle Bob is
turning 50!

Please join us
on Sept 1st to
help him
celebrate.

Over the Hill

Designer: Layle Koncar

ⓐ INVITATION

1. Make gatefold card from patterned paper.
2. Cut patterned paper panel; ink edges. Adhere to left card flap.
3. Adhere cardstock rectangle and patterned paper strip.
4. Print hill sentiment on patterned paper; trim, ink edges, and adhere with foam tape.
5. Print party details on patterned paper; trim, ink edges, and adhere inside card.

ⓑ BIRTHDAY TAG

1. Print hill sentiment on patterned paper. Punch into circle and ink edges.
2. Mat piece with patterned paper, using foam tape. Ink mat edges.
3. Attach brad to number stickers; adhere.

ⓒ ADVICE BOOK

1. Cover book with patterned paper; ink edges.
2. Tie on ribbon.
3. Print advice sentiment on patterned paper. Trim, ink edges, and adhere.

ⓓ NOISEMAKER

1. Adhere patterned paper to noisemaker cover; ink edges.
2. Print hill sentiment on patterned paper, punch into circle, ink edges, and adhere.

ⓔ PARTY HAT

1. Take apart party hat and trace on patterned paper. Trim and assemble patterned paper hat.
2. Trim patterned paper piece, ink edges, and adhere to hat.
3. Affix number stickers.
4. Punch holes in hat sides and tie on ribbon.
5. Trim vellum strips, curl ends, and adhere.

ⓕ FAVOR CONE

1. Cover cone with patterned paper.
2. Fill cone with candy, wrap with cellophane, and tie on ribbon.
3. Print thank you on patterned paper, punch into circle, and ink edges. Adhere to metal-rim tag and tie to ribbon.

ⓖ GIFT BOX

1. Cut patterned paper; adhere around box.
2. Adhere patterned paper strip.
3. Print old geezer on label; adhere.
4. Attach brads.

ⓗ PLACE MARKER

1. Print guest's name on label.
2. Affix label to pill bottle front.
3. Fill with candy.

ⓘ GLASS TAG

1. Print guest's name on patterned paper; punch into circle.
2. Ink circle edges. Adhere to punched patterned paper circle.
3. Punch hole at top of tag and attach to martini glass with ball chain.

Designer Tip

Sentiments from this party ensemble can be found on the included CD.

Try This

Have guests write advice to the birthday honoree in the advice book, then take their photos and add them to the book later.

THANK YOU

OVER THE HILL

¾ 5 ¼ ½ ¾ 6 ¼

BULLS EYE

SHOT

ADVICE ON GETTING OLDER

½ ¾ ¼ ½ ¾ 6 ¼

½ ¾ ¼ ½ ¾ 4 ¼ ½ ¾ 6 ¼

I'M OVER THE HILL

50

OVER THE HILL

HOLD TAB DOWN TURN

STEVE

OLD GEEZER

STEVE

(a) (b) (c) (d) (e) (f) (g) (h) (i)

Sweet Sixteen Celebration

Designer: Layle Koncar

(a) INVITATION

1. Make card from patterned paper; ink edges and draw border.
2. Cut patterned paper square, ink edges, and draw border. Mat with patterned paper and ink edges; adhere.
3. Affix stickers to spell sentiment; draw apostrophe.
4. Affix banner sticker and adhere rhinestones.

(b) MINI BOOK

1. Adhere patterned paper piece and strip to book. Draw border around piece.
2. Affix tape and adhere brads.
3. Apply banner rub-ons. Affix cake and candle.
4. Cut patterned paper piece, affix stickers to spell "Sweet 16", and adhere rhinestones. Adhere piece with foam tape.
5. Tie on ribbon.

(c) GIFT BAG

1. Affix ribbon stickers to bag. Adhere rhinestones.
2. Fold top of bag and punch holes, thread with ribbon, and tie bow.
3. Ink edges of canvas tag. Adhere button and affix monogram sticker.
4. Tie on tag with twine.

(d) CANDY BAR WRAP

1. Wrap candy bar with patterned paper.
2. Cut patterned paper strip, ink edges, and adhere to wrap.
3. Stamp thank you on patterned paper. Ink edges and adhere with foam tape.

(e) NAPKIN WRAP

1. Wrap plastic utensils in napkin. Tie on ribbon.
2. Adhere admit one sticker with foam tape.

(f) CENTERPIECE

1. Adhere patterned paper to bucket; affix lace and gift stickers.
2. Fill bucket with candy.
3. Back celebrate, pinwheel, and balloon stickers with patterned paper. Adhere to sticks.
4. Affix stars to balloon. Place sticks in bucket.

(g) CUPCAKE WRAPPER

1. Cut wrapper, following pattern found on CD.
2. Trim wrapper top with decorative-edge scissors, ink edges, and adhere wrapper ends.

(h) CUPCAKE TOPPER

1. Cut heart from patterned paper and adhere to food pick.
2. Ink edges and outline with pen.
3. Affix candle sticker.

(i) BOTTLE WRAP

1. Cut patterned paper strip and adhere around bottle.
2. Adhere balloon die cut with foam tape.
3. Affix stickers to spell guest name. Adhere rhinestone.

Try This

Use the mini book to capture photos and autographs from party guests.

Zoo Birthday

Designer: Lindsay Amrhein

ⓐ INVITATION

1. Make card from cardstock; adhere patterned paper.
2. Print party details on cardstock; trim. Mat with patterned paper and adhere.
3. Stamp giraffe on cardstock; color. Trim and adhere with foam tape.

ⓑ THANK YOU CARD

1. Make card from cardstock; adhere patterned paper.
2. Stamp animals on cardstock; color. Cut into square, mat with patterned paper, and adhere.
3. Die-cut circle from patterned paper. Die-cut and emboss circle from cardstock.
4. Stamp thanks sentiment on cardstock circle, mat with patterned paper circle, and adhere with foam tape.

ⓒ CUPCAKE TOPPERS

1. Die-cut stars from cardstock; adhere skewers.
2. Cut patterned paper strips. Die-cut patterned paper circles. Accordion-fold strips and adhere to circles. Adhere to stars.
3. Die-cut circles from patterned paper; adhere to toppers.
4. Stamp sentiment on cardstock, trim, notch ends, and adhere to one topper.
5. Stamp giraffe, hippo, and crocodile on cardstock; color. Cut out and adhere with foam tape.

ⓓ BANNER

1. Cut triangles from cardstock. Cut smaller triangles from patterned paper; adhere.
2. Border-punch edge of cardstock strips, adhere narrow cardstock strips, and adhere to triangles.
3. Punch scalloped circles from cardstock. Die-cut circles from cardstock, mat with scalloped circles, and adhere.
4. Stamp giraffe, crocodile, and hippo on cardstock; color. Cut out and adhere with foam tape.
5. Attach triangles with brads. Adhere twine to banner ends.

ⓔ TREAT BAG TOPPER

1. Make topper from cardstock.
2. Cut patterned paper strip; mat with cardstock and adhere.
3. Punch scalloped circle from patterned paper and adhere with foam tape.
4. Stamp desired animal on cardstock; color. Cut out and adhere.

Try This

Play charades! Have guests act out a zoo-ful of animals.

Guitar Hero Birthday

Designer: Lisa Johnson

ⓐ INVITATION

1. Make card from cardstock.
2. Cut patterned paper panel, round right corners, and adhere.
3. Cut cardstock panel; round right corners. Stamp music, guitar, and rock on!; color. Ink edges and adhere to card.
4. Cut patterned paper strip, trim with decorative-edge trimmer, and adhere. Tie on twine.
5. Die-cut stars from cardstock, stamp sheet music, and ink edges. Adhere, using foam tape for one.
6. Die-cut guitar from cardstock. Stamp guitar, color, and adhere with foam tape.

ⓑ BOTTLE WRAP

1. Cut patterned paper strip; adhere around bottle.
2. Die-cut star from cardstock.
3. Stamp you rock! on cardstock, color, and punch into circle. Ink edges, adhere to star, and adhere to bottle.
4. Die-cut guitar from cardstock. Stamp guitar, color, and adhere with foam tape.

ⓒ FOOD PICK

1. Die-cut star from cardstock.
2. Color toothpick and adhere to star.
3. Die-cut guitar from cardstock. Stamp guitar, color, and adhere.

ⓓ GIFT BAG

1. Cut patterned paper panel.
2. Stamp sheet music on cardstock, cut strips, and trim with decorative-edge trimmer. Ink edges and adhere to panel. Adhere panel to bag.
3. Die-cut stars from cardstock, stamp sheet music, and ink edges. Mat with stars die-cut from cardstock. Adhere.
4. Die-cut guitar from cardstock. Stamp guitar, color, and adhere with foam tape.
5. Stamp happy birthday; color. Trim, ink edges, and adhere with foam tape.

ⓔ CANDY BAR WRAP

1. Cut cardstock wrap.
2. Cut patterned paper strips, trim one with decorative-edge trimmer, and adhere to wrap.
3. Stamp music on wrap and adhere around candy bar.
4. Stamp sentiment on cardstock, color, trim, and adhere.
5. Stamp sheet music on cardstock, die-cut into star, ink edges, and adhere.
6. Die-cut guitar from cardstock. Stamp guitar, color, and adhere.

ⓕ FOOD HOLDER

1. Make holder, following pattern found on CD. Assemble.
2. Stamp sheet music on cardstock strip, cut with decorative-edge trimmer, and adhere.
3. Stamp you rock on cardstock, color, and punch into oval. Ink edges and adhere.
4. Stamp sheet music on cardstock, die-cut into star, and adhere with foam tape.

Designer Tip

When having a mixed-gender party for teens, make sure that the color scheme and design lean more toward masculine or neutral.

Try This

Have a Guitar Hero game competition and use the giant candy bar as first prize!

Cute Cupcake Party

Designer: Lucy Abrams

ⓐ CUPCAKE BOX

1. Trim cardstock panels to fit inside box sides. Stamp Raindrop Background and stitch and ink edges.
2. Assemble box and adhere panels inside.
3. Open cupcake in software, resize as desired, and print on cardstock. Trim, color, and apply dimensional glaze and glitter.
4. Adhere cupcakes. Tie on ribbon.

See inside image of box on p. 287.

ⓑ NAPKIN RING

1. Print guest name on cardstock. Stamp Raindrop Background, cut into strips, and stitch and ink edges.
2. Mat strips with cardstock. Adhere ends to make ring.
3. Open cupcake in software, resize as desired, and print on cardstock. Trim, color, and apply dimensional glaze and glitter.
4. Tie twine around cupcakes and adhere to rings with foam tape.

ⓒ CUPCAKE TOPPER

1. Open cupcake in software, resize as desired, and print on cardstock.
2. Trim cupcake, color, and apply dimensional glaze and glitter.
3. Print flavor on cardstock, stamp Raindrop Background, stitch, and trim into flag. Adhere behind cupcake.
4. Adhere cupcake to toothpick.

ⓓ INVITATION

1. Make card from cardstock.
2. Print sentiment on cardstock. Stamp Raindrop Background, stitch and ink edges, and adhere.
3. Open cupcake in software, resize as desired, and print on cardstock. Trim, color, and apply dimensional glaze and glitter.
4. Tie twine around one cupcake; adhere. Adhere remaining cupcakes.

ⓔ MENU

1. Print menu on cardstock.
2. Stamp Raindrop Background. Stitch and ink edges.
3. Border-punch cardstock strips; adhere behind menu.
4. Open cupcake in software, resize as desired, and print on cardstock. Trim, color, and apply dimensional glaze and glitter. Adhere to menu.

Designer Tip

Menu wording can be found on included CD.

Try This

Celebrate the joy of sweet treats by serving only cupcakes at your party.

ⓐ

ⓓ

it's
PARTY
time

Menu

Strawberry and Vanilla Marble Cake
with Vanilla Frosting
Topped with a Fresh Strawberry

~

Raspberry Ripple Cake
with White Chocolate Frosting
Decorated with Dark Chocolate Sprinkles

~

Coconut Cake
with Dark Chocolate Frosting
Dusted with Icing Sugar

~

Double Chocolate Cake
with Milk Chocolate Frosting

~

Lemon Cake
with Zesty Lemon Frosting

ⓔ

ⓒ

Coconut

Raspberry

Lemon

EMILY

ⓑ

Birthday Camp Out

Designer: Sarah Jay

(a) TOTE BAG

1. Print guest's name on transfer paper. Trim and iron on tote.
2. Adhere patch.

(b) BANNER

1. Cut flags from burlap; ink edges.
2. Cut patterned paper panels; adhere to flags.
3. Stamp fire, owl, fox, and log on cardstock. Stamp owl on patterned paper. Color images and trim; assemble owl.
4. Punch heart from patterned paper. Adhere to flag with foam tape. Adhere fire with foam tape.
5. Adhere stickers with foam tape across remaining flags to spell "I ♥ camping". Adhere owl and fox.
6. Attach flags to cord with clothespins.

(c) INVITATION

1. Cut cardstock to finished size base. Adhere patterned paper.
2. Cut tent from cardstock; score and cut flap. Cut cardstock to fit behind flap, color, and adhere behind tent.
3. Stamp "I ♥ camping" on cardstock; trim and distress edges. Cut cardstock strip, color, and adhere behind sign. Adhere sign and tent to panel. Punch heart from patterned paper and adhere.
4. Stamp raccoon on cardstock; color, trim, and adhere, using foam tape.
5. Print party details on cardstock; trim. Border-punch top and adhere.

(d) SNACK BAG

1. Cut cardstock to 4" x 3"; fold. Adhere patterned paper strip.
2. Stamp fire on cardstock; color, trim, and adhere.
3. Stamp "I ♥ s'mores". Punch heart from patterned paper and adhere.
4. Fill large glassine bag with snacks, fold top, and add topper. Punch holes and tie on twine.

(e) THANK YOU CARD

1. Make card from cardstock.
2. Cut patterned paper; adhere.
3. Stamp "Thanks friend!" on cardstock; trim and distress edges. Cut cardstock strip, color, and adhere to card. Adhere stamped piece.
4. Border-punch edge of cardstock strip; adhere. Adhere patterned paper strip.
5. Stamp dragonfly, owl, and log on cardstock. Stamp owl on patterned paper. Color images, trim, assemble owl, and adhere images to card with foam tape.

(f) DRINK HANGER

1. Cut cardstock to 2¼" x 8½"; score 2¼" from each end. Punch circle from one end and round top corners.
2. Fold bottom end up and adhere patterned paper strip. Punch holes and tie on twine.
3. Stamp sentiment. Punch heart from patterned paper; adhere.
4. Stamp dragonfly on cardstock, color, trim, and adhere.

(g) PHOTO ALBUM

1. Cut cardstock panel to fit inside album cover; round bottom corners.
2. Cut slightly smaller piece of patterned paper; adhere.
3. Cut tent from cardstock; score and cut flap. Cut cardstock to fit behind flap, color, and adhere behind tent.
4. Stamp sentiment on cardstock; trim and distress edges. Cut cardstock strip, color, and adhere behind sign. Adhere sign and tent to panel.
5. Stamp raccoon, fire, and camera on cardstock; color, trim, and adhere, using foam tape for camera.
6. Border-punch cardstock strip, round bottom corners, and adhere to panel. Insert panel in album cover.

(h) BADGE FAVOR

1. Punch brad toppers from patterned paper; attach to jumbo brads.
2. Remove brad prongs and adhere pin backs.
3. Affix star sticker to one brad. Apply decoupage finish; let dry.
4. Cut tag from cardstock. Punch patterned paper circle, adhere, punch hole, and thread with twine.
5. Adhere brad badges with repositionable adhesive.
6. Stamp "For you" and fox on small glassine bag; heat-set. Insert tag.

See inside image of badge favor on p. 282

(i) CUPCAKE WRAP & TOPPERS

1. Cut wrapper from patterned paper, following pattern found on CD. Adhere ends.
2. Stamp fox and owl on cardstock. Stamp owl on patterned paper. Stamp logs on cardstock. Color fox and owl, trim all pieces, and adhere together. Adhere sticks.
3. Stamp fox and owl on patterned paper; trim. Stamp logs on cardstock; trim. Adhere behind toppers.

Designer Tip

Use the threads in burlap as cutting guides to get straighter lines. Invitation wording can be found on included CD.

Try This

Serve traditional camping fare like hot dogs, roasted marshmallows, and lemonade. Bring in a portable fire pit or small camp stoves for roasting marshmallows.

Ⓐ

Ⓑ

Ⓒ

CAMP

Ⓒ

I ♥ camping

We're camping under the stars for
CHARLIE'S 6th
BIRTHDAY

Join us for a
backyard camping adventure
Saturday, August 8 at 6pm
Pick-up Sunday at 10am

Camp Charlie
15 Forrest Avenue

Don't forget to pack your
flashlight, toothbrush,
sleeping bag, pillow,
and a change of clothes.

Ⓐ

THOMAS

you're such a deer

I ♥ s'mores

Ⓓ

Ⓕ

I bug juice

Ⓘ

Ⓔ

thanks friend!

for you

Ⓗ

I campfire memories

Ⓖ

Little Cowboy Roundup

Designer: Sarah Martina Parker

ⓐ INVITATION

1. Cut patterned paper panel to finished size.
2. Stamp journaling block on cardstock; trim and round corners. Stamp Designer Woodgrain.
3. Stamp date, time, place, rsvp, and cowboy. Adhere to panel and staple.
4. Die-cut label from patterned paper; stamp frame. Thread buttons; adhere. Stamp birthday shindig on cardstock, trim, and adhere with foam tape. Adhere label to panel with foam tape.
5. Stamp boots, trim, and adhere to ticket sticker with foam tape. Affix sticker.

ⓑ FOOD PICK

1. Stamp vittles title on cardstock; trim.
2. Cut mats from cardstock, adhere glitter, and adhere title with foam tape.
3. Adhere piece to toothpicks. Fill pail with gift shred and insert picks.

ⓒ EYE PATCH

1. Cut patterned paper square; round corners.
2. Stamp yee haw on cardstock, trim, and adhere glitter. Adhere to square and zigzag-stitch edge.
3. Cut slit down center of square, overlap edges, and adhere.
4. Punch holes in sides of patch and tie on twine.

ⓓ FRAME

1. Cut patterned paper to 3" x 9¼". Score at 1", 4½", and 8¼"; fold and adhere ends.
2. Adhere patterned paper rectangle. Adhere photo and tie on twine.
3. Stamp wanted frame on patterned paper; trim around and cut out center. Ink edges and adhere with foam tape.
4. Die-cut star from cardstock, adhere glitter, and adhere with foam tape. Thread button and adhere.

ⓔ NAPKIN RING

1. Cut patterned paper strip; stamp star borders.
2. Mat strip with cardstock and border-punch mat edges.
3. Stamp sheriff's star on cardstock; trim and ink edges. Cut mat from cardstock, adhere glitter, and adhere star with foam tape. Adhere to strip.
4. Attach brads. Adhere ends of strip together to form ring.

ⓕ SHERIFF'S BADGE

1. Die-cut star from cardstock and adhere glitter.
2. Stamp cowboy on cardstock, trim, and adhere with foam tape.
3. Stamp stars on cardstock, cut out, and adhere.
4. Adhere safety pin to star back.

ⓖ PLACE CARD

1. Make card from patterned paper; stamp star border.
2. Die-cut boot from cardstock; assemble and stitch. Ink edges and adhere.
3. Affix stickers to spell guest's name; adhere with foam tape.
4. Attach twine with clothespins.

Designer Tip

When using a fairly neutral color palette, add extra interest by incorporating lots of bling and glitter.

Try This

Make the party even more fun with costumes. Suggest guests wear boots, cowboy hats, bandanas, and vests.

(a)

(d)

(c)

(b)

(f)

(g)

(e)

BIRTHDAY
SHINDIG

date
time
place
rsvp

WANTED

REWARD
$500 CASH

YEE ★ HAW

Sweet Celebration

Designer: Sarah Martina Parker

ⓐ INVITATION

1. Make card from cardstock.
2. Cut patterned paper, die-cut lace border, and adhere. Zigzag-stitch sides.
3. Cut patterned paper panel; trim top with decorative-edge scissors. Adhere ribbon and wrap with twine. Mat panel with patterned paper.
4. Stamp frame on cardstock. Stamp birthday party. Trim and adhere to panel with foam tape. Adhere panel to card with foam tape.
5. Adhere lollipop sticker with foam tape; adhere pearl. Thread button with twine and adhere.

ⓑ CUPCAKE WRAPPERS & STANDS

1. Print template on cardstock; trim.
2. Print template on patterned paper; trim into strips. Trim top edges with decorative-edge scissors and adhere to cardstock pieces; zigzag-stitch.
3. Adhere ends together.
4. Paint stands; let dry. Assemble.

ⓒ HAIR CLIP GIFT

1. Die-cut button card from cardstock; cut two vertical slits, one above the other, in center of card.
2. Die-cut label from patterned paper. Die-cut hanger slot from label. Cut slit to match card and adhere behind card. Tie on twine.
3. Die-cut two large and four medium flowers from felt. Fold each medium flower in half twice; stitch bottom.
4. Layer large flowers; adhere together. Adhere folded flowers. Thread button with twine; adhere.
5. Cut leaves from felt; adhere to flower. Adhere ribbon to clip and adhere flower.
6. Repeat Steps 3-5 to create second clip, substituting fabric brad for button.
7. Slide clips through slits on card.

ⓓ BANNER

1. Stitch doilies together.
2. Affix doily stickers.
3. Tie seam binding bows; adhere. Adhere pearls.
4. Spray silhouettes with ink; let dry. Adhere.
5. Tie twine bows, adhere to ends of banner, and attach clothespins.

ⓔ THANK YOU CARD

1. Make card from cardstock.
2. Cut patterned paper and die-cut scalloped border from one edge.
3. Adhere doily. Affix border sticker. Tie on twine and adhere to card.
4. Affix border stickers to journaling block; zigzag-stitch one seam. Adhere border sticker with foam tape. Attach brad and adhere block to card with foam tape.
5. Stamp frame and thank you on cardstock. Trim and adhere.
6. Adhere chipboard flower. Thread button with twine and adhere.

ⓕ NAME TAG

1. Die-cut scalloped circle from patterned paper.
2. Print guest names on patterned paper; punch into circle. Adhere to scalloped circle and punch hole.
3. Adhere buttons. Affix floral circle sticker.
4. Tie tag to lollipop with twine.

Designer Tip

Using spray ink to color chipboard shapes is a great alternative to painting because it dries much faster.

Try This

Entertain party guests with cupcake decorating stations.

Manly Man Party Time

Designer: Teri Anderson

ⓐ INVITATION

1. Tear cardboard rectangle.
2. Print party details on cardstock. Trim, adhere to cardboard, and affix tape.

ⓑ THANK YOU NOTE

1. Tear cardboard rectangle.
2. Print thank you note on cardstock. Trim, adhere to cardboard, and affix tape.
3. Check boxes and sign with marker.

ⓒ STEIN MARKER

1. Tear piece of cardboard.
2. Cut small triangle in center of bottom edge.
3. Write guest name.

ⓓ PLACEMAT

1. Tear cardboard rectangle.
2. Affix tape.

ⓔ FAVOR

1. Tear cardboard strip; adhere around screw box.
2. Print "Thanks for coming, man!" on cardstock. Trim, distress slightly, and adhere. Affix tape.

ⓕ FOOD MARKER

1. Tear pieces of cardboard.
2. Print "Man grub" on cardstock. Trim, distress, and adhere to cardboard. Affix tape.
3. Adhere stick behind cardboard and wrap with tape.

Designer Tip

The cheaper, the better for this party. Instead of cracking into a new box for the ensemble, recycle old boxes for cardboard pieces.

(a)

Bob's turning 40,
and we're celebrating with a Manly Man party.

It will be a party where burping is encouraged,
football is talked about
and muscles are flexed.

The party begins at 7 p.m. Friday.
Beer and man grub will be served.

RSVP: 555-1212

(f)

Man grub

(e)

Thanks for coming, man!   Thanks for coming, man!

(b)

Hey, man!
Thanks for:
X Coming to my party!
X Cracking a beer with me and talking football!
X For the practical gift!
Big thanks,
BOB

(c)

Ben

(d)

Poker Night!

Designer: Tiffany Johnson

(a) INVITATION & ENVELOPE

1. Print party details on cardstock; trim to finished size.
2. Adhere strip of transparency sheet. Affix tape.
3. Make envelope from patterned paper.
4. Die-cut game board from patterned paper. Die-cut circle from cardstock; adhere behind game board.
5. Stamp symbols on game board.
6. Die-cut spinner from patterned paper. Attach to game board with brad. Adhere game board to envelope flap.

(b) COASTERS

1. Die-cut heart, diamond, spade, and club from vinyl; adhere to coasters.
2. Stamp matching symbols on coasters.

(c) DRINK COZY

1. Die-cut band from foam.
2. Die-cut smaller band from transparency sheet.
3. Apply moustache rub-on.
4. Layer bands and attach eyelets. Tie to bottle with twine.

(d) DARE CARD

1. Print title on cardstock; trim to finished size.
2. Adhere patterned paper.
3. Die-cut game board from patterned paper. Die-cut circle from cardstock; adhere behind game board.
4. Stamp numbers on game board.
5. Die-cut spinner from patterned paper. Attach to game board with brad. Adhere game board to card.

(e) MOUSTACHES

1. Apply moustache rub-ons to cardstock; trim.
2. Adhere moustaches to skewers.
3. Apply moustache rub-on to small bucket. Fill bucket with floral foam and gift shred; insert moustaches.

(f) BANNER

1. Print "Poker" letters on cardstock. Die-cut and emboss into pennants.
2. Die-cut tabbed pennants from transparency sheets, cardstock, and patterned paper.
3. Adhere transparency pennants to cardstock and patterned paper pennants. Adhere printed pennants.
4. Die-cut diamond and club from vinyl; adhere to pennants.
5. Set eyelets in pennant tabs. String pennants on twine to form banner.

(g) CENTERPIECE

1. Die-cut eight pennants of various sizes from patterned paper.
2. Adhere larger pennants to cardstock for stability; trim.
3. Adhere pennants to dowels.
4. Die-cut spade from vinyl; adhere to bucket. Fill bucket with floral foam and gift shred; insert pennants.

(h) FOOD PICKS

1. Die-cut picks from acrylic sheet.
2. Print food labels on cardstock; die-cut into labels.
3. Affix tape across picks. Adhere labels.

Designer Tip

Make it a competition! Provide a trophy for the winner to go along with the bragging rights. Invite and "dare card" sentiments can be found on included CD.

Cirque du Soleil Birthday

Designer: Vanessa Menhorn

ⓐ BANNER

1. Cut cardboard base. Cut crepe paper strips, layer, fold top end in half, and adhere fold to cardboard. Repeat.
2. At half crepe paper length, stitch strips together. *Note: Do not pull straight, allow strips to hang loose.* Repeat with other side strips.
3. Cut small cardstock circles. Staple ribbon to form loops. Adhere to top of stitched crepe sides for hanging.
4. Cut patterned paper strips, accordion-fold, and adhere together. Adhere to base.
5. Die-cut circle from patterned paper. Mat with scalloped circle die-cut from cardstock.
6. Open clown face in software, resize as desired, and print on cardstock. Fussy-cut and adhere to circle. Adhere circle with foam tape.

ⓑ INVITATION

1. Cut patterned paper panel.
2. Cut crepe paper strip, fold twice, and adhere top edge to panel; zigzag-stitch. Trim fringe.
3. Border-punch edge of cardstock strip; adhere bottom edge to panel. Tie on twine and adhere panel to card.
4. Print sentiment on cardstock; trim into flag and curl slightly. Adhere to skewer, tuck into border, and adhere.
5. Cut ticket from patterned paper; tuck into border.

ⓒ CUPCAKE TOPPER

1. Cut rectangle from patterned paper; notch bottom.
2. Open clown in software, resize as desired, and print on cardstock. Fussy-cut and adhere with foam tape.
3. Roll crepe paper strip and adhere.
4. Adhere rectangle to skewer.

ⓓ POPCORN CONE

1. Cut 6" square piece of patterned paper. Roll diagonally and adhere.
2. Cut crepe paper strip, roll tightly, and adhere to cone.

ⓔ BOTTLE & STRAW WRAPS

1. Cut crepe paper length; adhere around bottle.
2. Cut patterned paper strip; adhere.
3. Cut tickets from patterned paper, fold around straw, and adhere.

Designer Tip

The tickets in the invitations are not adhered so your guests can bring their tickets for admission to the party.

Try This

Set up a photo booth with fun props like moustaches on sticks, red clown noses, and oversized glasses.

Sweet Girl Birthday

Designer: Wendy Sue Anderson

ⓐ BANNER

1. Die-cut scalloped banner flags and tops from patterned paper. Die-cut banner flags from cardstock.
2. Emboss banner flags, ink, and stitch edges. Adhere to scalloped flags.
3. Die-cut "Party" from patterned paper, using font. Adhere letters with foam tape.
4. Attach eyelets to banner tops, stitch top edges, and adhere to flags with foam tape.
5. Tie flags together with ribbon.

ⓑ CENTERPIECE

1. Cover mirror frame with patterned paper.
2. Paint lollipop sticks; let dry.
3. Die-cut seven layered flowers from patterned paper; curl edges slightly. Adhere flowers to lollipop sticks.
4. Thread buttons with crochet thread and adhere to flower centers.
5. Place flowers in vases and arrange on mirror.

ⓒ TABLE RUNNER

1. Cut patterned paper strips in varying widths. *Note: Cut two of each size in each pattern.*
2. Stitch strips to left and right sides of patterned paper sheet, varying stitches as desired.

ⓓ FAVOR BAG

1. Die-cut purse from patterned paper.
2. Attach eyelets to purse top, tie on ribbon, and assemble purse.
3. Trim sentiment block from patterned paper. Mat with patterned paper and adhere with foam tape.
4. Include patterned paper wrapped lip balm and a mimi candy bar as part of the favors.

ⓔ FRAME

1. Paint frame; let dry.
2. Cover with patterned paper.
3. Adhere patterned paper inside frame.
4. Affix flower sticker. Thread button with crochet thread and adhere.

ⓕ CANDY TUBES

1. Cut sentiment labels from patterned paper; attach eyelets.
2. Tie labels to tubes with ribbon.
3. Fill tubes with candy.

ⓖ BARRETTE

1. Cover barrette top with patterned paper.
2. Die-cut layered flower from patterned paper; adhere to barrette.
3. Thread button with crochet thread; adhere.

See detailed image of barrette on p. 287.

ⓗ THANK YOU TAG & RING

1. Cut tag from patterned paper; attach eyelet.
2. Die-cut layered flower from patterned paper; adhere.
3. Adhere crochet thread behind flower and tie to ring. Adhere rhinestone.
4. Tie ring to tag with crochet thread.

See detailed image of tag & ring on p. 287.

ⓘ GIFT BOX

1. Die-cut box from patterned paper; assemble.
2. Cut ¾" strips of patterned paper at three different lengths. Adhere ends of strips to form loops.
3. Adhere loops to box top to form bow.
4. Adhere doily and flower stickers in center of bow, using foam tape. Thread button with crochet thread and adhere.
5. Cut sentiment block from patterned paper and adhere.

ⓙ INVITATION & ENVELOPE

1. Make tri-fold card from cardstock.
2. Adhere patterned paper to card flaps.
3. Cut patterned paper strip, fold around card, and adhere ends. Print "...to my birthday party!" on cardstock, trim, and adhere.
4. Cut doily circle from patterned paper; adhere. Affix doily sticker. Thread button with crochet thread and adhere.
5. Die-cut envelope from patterned paper; assemble. Thread button sticker with crochet thread and affix to flap.
6. Print "Are invited" on patterned paper; trim, stitch edge, and adhere to envelope. Affix you.

ⓚ CUPCAKE WRAPPERS & TOPPERS

1. Die-cut cupcake wrappers from patterned paper; assemble.
2. Punch circles from patterned paper; staple to wrappers. Adhere purse stickers with foam tape.
3. Affix silhouette stickers to craft sticks to form toppers.

At Home Spa Day

Designer: Julie Campbell

(a) INVITATION

1. Make card from cardstock.
2. Cut patterned paper panel. Stitch, ink, and distress edges.
3. Tie on tulle. Adhere rhinestone. Adhere panel to card.
4. Print invitation on cardstock; trim and adhere to panel.
5. Ink edges of frame sticker; affix. Adhere nail polish sticker with foam tape.

(b) WRAPPED TOWEL

1. Cut cardstock strip to fit around folded towel; double-stitch edges.
2. Adhere ribbon. Stitch on button.
3. Affix hook and loop fastener to ends of strip. Wrap around towel and secure.

(c) FLIP FLOPS

1. Adhere patterned paper to sides of flip flops.
2. Adhere flowers.

(d) BATH SALTS

1. Adhere ribbon around jar.
2. Print "Bath salts" on cardstock; die-cut into circle.
3. Stamp doily on circle, ink edges, and adhere to doily with foam tape. Adhere to jar.
4. Fill jar with bath salts.

(e) WATER BOTTLE

1. Adhere patterned paper strip around bottle.
2. Adhere pompom trim.
3. Adhere flower sticker with foam tape. Affix floral circle sticker to cap.

(f) SPA SUPPLIES CONTAINER

1. Cover box with patterned paper; adhere lace.
2. Affix flower sticker. Place tulle inside.

(g) FAVOR BUCKET

1. Adhere ribbon around bucket.
2. Print sentiment on cardstock; die-cut into circle.
3. Stamp doily on circle, ink edges, and adhere to bucket with foam tape.
4. Place tulle inside.

Designer Tip

Spa parties aren't just for little girls! Invite your own friends over for a girlfriends or moms spa day. Invite wording an be found on included CD.

Try This

- Create frozen fruity drinks and top them with umbrella picks for a fun spa beverage.

- Send each girl home with a bucket filled with nail polish, scented lip balm, or travel sized lotions.

- Host a birthday slumber party and invite girls to arrive in their most comfy pajamas. They'll be ready for their spa treatment as soon as they arrive!

- Provide decorated flip flops for each girl. These are very inexpensive and are perfect for post-pedicure feet.

g

c

e

b

A gift
for you

Bath
Salts

d

f

a

Join us for a
Spa Party
To celebrate Anna's 6th birthday!

Graduation

Designer: Renae Curtz

(a) ACCORDION DÉCOR

1. Cut eight 3¾" x 4¾" chipboard panels; cover with cardstock.
2. Pierce circle on four panels.
3. Cut patterned paper strips; adhere to non-pierced panels. Punch circles from patterned paper and adhere.
4. Thread buttons with linen thread and adhere to non-pierced panels.
5. Die-cut "Congrats" from cardstock. Adhere to panels with foam tape.
6. Cut cardstock strips and adhere behind panels to connect.

(b) INVITATION

1. Cut two cardstock squares. Cut strip of cardstock, accordion-fold, and adhere between squares.
2. Cut tag from cardstock; punch circle. Stamp time to and celebrate. Stamp time to on cardstock, trim, and adhere to tag with foam tape.
3. Make tassel from floss.
4. Thread button with floss. Adhere tassel, tag, and button to invitation.
5. Punch half-circle from invitation edge to hold tassel.

(c) FRAME

1. Cut patterned paper to fit frame, round corners, and adhere.
2. Tie on ribbon.
3. Cut tag from cardstock. Cut monogram from patterned paper and adhere with foam tape.
4. Adhere button to tag. Adhere tag to frame.

(d) CARD

1. Make card from cardstock.
2. Adhere patterned paper; pierce.
3. Stamp congratulations; emboss.
4. Cut letters from patterned paper to spell "Grad"; adhere with foam tape.
5. Thread button with linen thread; adhere.

(e) FAVOR BOX

1. Die-cut box from cardstock; assemble.
2. Cut patterned paper strip; adhere around box. Adhere ribbon.
3. Cut cardstock tag, stamp good times, and adhere to box with foam tape.
4. Thread button with linen thread; adhere.

Designer Tip

Change the color scheme to reflect the graduate's school colors.

Off to College

Designer: Joannie McBride

ⓐ CARD

❶ Affix label sticker to card.
❷ Affix stickers to spell "Off to college".

ⓑ GIFT CARD

❶ Trim square from card and adhere to bag.
❷ Affix stickers to spell "Gift card".
❸ Insert gift card and tie on twine.

ⓒ NOTEBOOK

❶ Cut cardstock panel, ink edges, and adhere to notebook.
❷ Cut patterned paper panel. Trim card and adhere to panel.
❸ Adhere ribbon. Adhere panel to notebook.
❹ Affix stickers to spell "Notes".

ⓓ MAC 'N CHEESE & CEREAL WRAPS

❶ Cut patterned paper strips; adhere around boxes.
❷ Adhere ribbon.
❸ Tie on twine.

ⓔ PEANUT BUTTER & JELLY WRAPS

❶ Cut patterned paper strips; adhere around jars.
❷ Adhere ribbon.
❸ Tie on twine.

ⓕ CANDY JAR

❶ Cut patterned paper strip; adhere around jar.
❷ Affix note square sticker; tie on twine.
❸ Tie on ribbon.

Try This

Include this fun ensemble with a small appliance like a toaster or a coffee maker.

Back to School

Designer: Angie Tieman

ⓐ PHOTO GARLAND

1. Paint doilies; let dry.
2. Cut patterned paper panels, adhere to lunch bags, and zigzag-stitch edges. Fold up bag bottoms and adhere left and right edges to form pockets. Insert overlay cards.
3. Tear muslin strip. Stitch to bag tops.
4. Fold doilies and adhere over bag tops. Die-cut starburst circles from patterned paper, fold, and adhere.
5. Stitch buttons to bags with twine. Insert photos behind overlay cards.

ⓑ BINGO BOARD

1. Paint frame; let dry.
2. Trim magnet sheet to fit inside frame; adhere. Cover with patterned paper.
3. Cut bingo card from patterned paper; cut off title. Adhere card inside frame; adhere patterned paper strip.
4. Die-cut scalloped border from felt; adhere. Thread canvas triangles on twine; adhere.
5. Punch hole in title strip, thread with twine, and tie to frame handle. Adhere strip to frame. Tie on twill.
6. Adhere circle magnets to buttons; place on board.

ⓒ SPELLING BOARD

1. Trim magnet sheet to fit inside cookie sheet; adhere.
2. Cut patterned paper to fit, round outside corners, and adhere.
3. Tear strip of muslin, gather, and adhere.
4. Affix alphabet stickers to magnet sheet, cut out, and place on board.

ⓓ TEACHER'S PENCIL JAR

1. Cut patterned paper strips and adhere around candle holder.
2. Tear muslin strip, paint, and let dry. Tie on.
3. Affix stickers to ticket to spell "Thanks". Cut teacher from patterned paper and adhere with foam tape.
4. Punch hole in ticket, string on twine, and tie twine around pencils. Place in jar.

ⓔ ENCOURAGEMENT NOTE

1. Cut bottoms from lunch bag. Adhere side flaps and zigzag-stitch bag bottom.
2. Affix stickers.
3. Cut quote card from patterned paper. Adhere ribbon loop.
4. Stitch button to cards with twine.
5. Insert card in bag.

Try this

- Get your kids excited and ready for back-to-school. Invite other moms and kids to make these fun projects!

- Use the Bingo Board to encourage reading. Every night your child reads a book to you, they can place a button on a bingo number. Once they get bingo, reward them with a small prize, like a cool pencil or a new book.

- Keep encouragement cards ready to go on days when your kids need a little extra boost, like a testing day.

Congrats on a Great Season!

Designer: Laura O'Donnell

ⓐ CENTERPIECE

❶ Cut foam block to fit in bucket; insert. Top with gift shred.

❷ Open play ball circle in software, resize to 4½" diameter, and print on photo paper. Trim and distress edges.

❸ Cut two 4¾" diameter circles from cardstock; adhere together over skewer. Adhere play ball circle and insert in bucket.

ⓑ DRINK WRAP

❶ Create finished size project in software. Drop in patterned paper and print on photo paper; trim.

❷ Open play ball circle in software, resize to 2¼" diameter, and print on photo paper. Trim, distress edges, and adhere to wrap.

❸ Adhere around water bottle.

ⓒ CUPCAKE TOPPER

❶ Stamp pennants on cardstock; trim.

❷ Stamp sentiment on one pennant.

❸ Adhere sentiment and blank pennant together over toothpicks.

ⓓ FOOD PICK

❶ Stamp star circles on cardstock; punch into circles.

❷ Adhere circles together over toothpicks.

ⓔ CARD

❶ Make card from cardstock.

❷ Print patterned paper on photo paper. Trim, distress edges, and adhere to card.

❸ Open ball game journal block and bat in software. Resize as desired, print on photo paper, trim, and adhere to card. *Note: Adhere journal block on three sides to form gift card pocket.*

❹ Stamp super star.

❺ Print "Coach" on cardstock. Fussy-cut letters and adhere using foam tape.

Designer Tip

Laura created a large coach's card to allow room for everyone on the team to sign and add personal messages inside.

Try this

Match the team colors with your ink and cardstock.

Urban Chic Engagement

Designer: Andrea Bowden, courtesy of Stampin' Up!

ⓐ INVITATION

❶ Create finished size trifold card project in software.

❷ On one panel, drop in cardstock, type invitation details, and change text opacity to 30%. Change color of couple's names. Insert plane icon.

❸ On another panel, insert icons and text.

❹ Fill remaining panels with paper and photos.

❺ Print on cardstock, trim, and fold.

ⓑ BOTTLE TAG

❶ Create finished size tag project in software.

❷ Drop in paper and add circle. Stamp dotted circle.

❸ Type sentiment and add plane icon.

❹ For tag back page, drop in cardstock, type wedding details, and change text opacity to 30%. Change color of couple's names.

❺ Print tag on cardstock, trim, and punch hole. Thread with ribbon.

ⓒ ALBUM

❶ Create finished size swatchbook project in software.

❷ For title page, drop in strips of cardstock and type couple's names.

❸ For remaining pages, drop in cardstock, patterned paper, and photos as desired.

❹ Print on album pages. Emboss bottom of title page and assemble album.

ⓓ FOOD PICKS

❶ Create desired size project in software.

❷ Add plane icon repeatedly, changing colors as desired.

❸ Print on cardstock and punch into circles. Adhere to toothpicks.

ⓔ PINWHEELS

❶ Print paper and digital cardstock on cardstock. *Note: Change opacity of digital cardstock to 50%.*

❷ Cut three 5½" squares from cardstock and printed cardstock. Cut diagonal slits from corners to 1" from square centers.

❸ Curl edges to square centers and attach brads to form pinwheels.

❹ Adhere pinwheels to dowels. Insert gift shred and pinwheels in vase.

ⓕ VASE BAND

❶ Create 12" x 2" project in software.

❷ Drop in cardstock strips.

❸ Type text, change opacity to 30%, change color of couple's names, and print on cardstock.

❹ Trim and adhere around vase.

ⓖ COASTER

❶ Open 4" square project in software.

❷ Stamp dotted circle and resize to 3¼".

❸ Type sentiment and add plane icon.

❹ Print on cardstock and die-cut into circle.

See detailed image of coaster on p. 287.

Try this

Print and punch extra food pick toppers to use as confetti on the party table.

Celebrating Romance

Designer: Melissa Phillips

ⓐ INVITATION

Ink all paper edges.

1. Make card from vellum; round right corners.
2. Cut patterned paper panel, trim with decorative-edge scissors, and adhere. Cut patterned paper strip and adhere.
3. Die-cut tag from cardstock. Stamp label and you're invited; adhere. Thread button with twine and adhere.
4. Adhere circle die cut. Notch ends of ribbon; adhere. Adhere vintage bride sticker with foam tape.
5. Ink resin heart and adhere with foam tape. Tie seam binding double bow; adhere. Adhere pearl.

ⓑ THANK YOU CARD

Ink all paper edges.

1. Make card from vellum; round right corners.
2. Cut patterned paper piece; adhere. Adhere floral trim.
3. Stamp thank you on tag and tie on seam binding. Thread button with twine, adhere, and adhere tag to card.
4. Adhere stamp sticker with foam tape.

ⓒ GUEST BOOK

Ink all paper edges.

1. Cut patterned paper panel. Adhere patterned paper strips.
2. Adhere label die cut and floral trim. Apply rub-on.
3. Punch panel edge to match album cover and adhere.
4. Adhere brides sticker with foam tape. Adhere flower.
5. Thread button with twine and adhere.

ⓓ FAVOR CONE

1. Print template on paper and trace on patterned paper; trim and assemble. Ink top edges.
2. Adhere tissue garland and tie on seam binding.
3. Ink edges of star die cut and adhere. Adhere floral sprig.
4. Ink resin heart and adhere. Adhere floral trim.

ⓔ PLACE CARD

Ink all paper edges.

1. Affix stamp sticker to tag.
2. Print name on vintage sheet music, trim, and adhere.
3. Adhere floral sprig and tie on seam binding.
4. Thread tag with ribbon. Thread button with twine and tie to ribbon.

ⓕ NAPKIN RING

1. Ink edges of oval die cut; punch ends and tie together with seam binding.
2. Adhere brooch.

ⓖ BANNER

1. Die-cut large banner flags from vellum.
2. Die-cut medium banner flags from patterned paper; ink edges and adhere to vellum flags.
3. Ink edges of die cuts and adhere die cuts, lace, floral trim, and ribbon to flags.
4. Spell "Love" with alphabet across flags. Adhere flower to one flag.
5. Thread pendants with twine and adhere. Cut pompoms from trim and adhere.
6. Punch tops of flags and tie together with seam binding.

Try this

The pattern for the Victorian paper cone can be downloaded at www.brendawalton.com/blog/files/victorian_paper_cone_template1.pdf.

Romantic Wedding Shower

Designer: Ashley Cannon Newell

ⓐ JOURNAL

1. Trim patterned paper and punch left edge. Adhere.
2. Trim strip of burlap and adhere.
3. Trim strip of cardstock, ink, and stamp love notes. Adhere.
4. Punch scalloped circles from patterned paper, crumple, and adhere together to create flowers; adhere.

ⓑ PLACE CARD

1. Stamp text background on cardstock and trim.
2. Die-cut large leaf from cardstock, stamp guest name, and ink edges. Adhere.
3. Die-cut small leaf from cardstock, stamp love blooms, and ink edges. Adhere.
4. Punch scalloped circles from patterned paper, crumple, and adhere together to create flower. Adhere.

See detailed image of the Place Card on p. 282

ⓒ THANK YOU CARD

1. Make card from cardstock.
2. Trim patterned paper and adhere.
3. Trim burlap and adhere. Zigzag-stitch edges.
4. Die-cut tag from cardstock, stamp love blooms, and ink edges. Adhere with foam tape.
5. Punch scalloped circles from patterned paper, crumple, and adhere together to create flowers; adhere.

ⓓ INVITATION

1. Make card from cardstock.
2. Trim patterned paper and mat with cardstock. Adhere panel and zigzag-stitch edges.
3. Trim burlap and adhere.
4. Stamp wedding and shower on cardstock, trim, and ink edges. Adhere.
5. Punch scalloped circles from patterned paper, crumple, and adhere together to create flowers; adhere.

ⓔ GIFT BOX

1. Die-cut box from cardstock.
2. Assemble and adhere.
3. Circle punch two sides, thread twine, and tie knots.
4. Die-cut tag from cardstock and stamp tag and thanks. Thread with twine and tie on.
5. Punch scalloped circles from patterned paper, crumple, and adhere together to create flower. Adhere.

See detailed image of Gift Box on p. 282

ⓕ NAPKIN RINGS

1. Trim burlap strip and adhere ends together.
2. Punch scalloped circles from patterned paper, crumple, and adhere together to create flower. Adhere.

ⓖ JAR

1. Trim strip of patterned paper and adhere.
2. Trim strip of burlap and adhere around jar.
3. Die-cut tag from cardstock, stamp love blooms, and ink edges. Thread with twine and tie around jar.
4. Punch scalloped circles from patterned paper, crumple, and adhere together to create flowers; adhere.

Designer Tip

When creating layered flowers, punch through multiple sheets of paper to create them faster.

d

c

g

a

f

e

b

CRAZY LOVE

wedding shower

Love NOTES

LAUREN

Kitchen Wedding Shower

Designer: Becky Olsen

ⓐ NAPKIN RING

❶ Trim strip of patterned paper.
❷ Trim strip of tulle and adhere.
❸ Trim strip of patterned paper, mat with patterned paper, and adhere to tulle. Adhere ends together to create ring.
❹ Punch conversation bubble from patterned paper and adhere with foam tape.

ⓑ TREAT BAG

❶ Trim patterned paper.
❷ Adhere into tube. Adhere ends in opposite directions.
❸ Tie on tulle.
❹ Punch tag from patterned paper and adhere.

ⓒ FOOD PICK

❶ Punch tag from patterned paper. Apply rub-ons to spell food name.
❷ Adhere toothpick.
❸ Tie bow with tulle and adhere to backside.

ⓓ BOTTLE WRAP

❶ Punch tag from patterned paper; attach brad.
❷ Adhere tulle and tie to bottle.

ⓔ INVITATION

❶ Trim strip of patterned paper and adhere to card.
❷ Punch scalloped circle from patterned paper, apply rub-ons to spell sentiment, and adhere inside card window.
❸ Wrap tulle and tie bow.
❹ Adhere button.

ⓕ THANK YOU CARD

❶ Punch tag from patterned paper; apply rub-ons to spell "Thank you".
❷ Attach spatula brad and adhere to patterned paper rectangle. Adhere to card.
❸ Tie bow with tulle and adhere with foam tape.
❹ Adhere button.

ⓖ ADVICE ALBUM

❶ Punch scalloped half-circle from patterned paper; apply rub-ons to spell sentiment. Adhere to album cover page and trim.
❸ Using binding machine and wire, bind all pages.
❹ Punch tags from patterned paper; Apply rub-ons to spell sentiments, trim, and adhere to tabs.
❺ Tie on tulle.

Designer Tip

Using pre-made cards for the invitations, thank you cards, and mini albums saves a lot of time.

Bonus Idea

This party ensemble could be created in many different themes. Look for die cuts that fit the theme you are working on and let the fun product do all of the heavy lifting.

b

yummy

fresh fruit

thank you

family recipe

d

e

a kitchen bridal shower

love

helpful hints and words of advice

key lime pie

c

f

g

a

Wedding Shower at the Beach

Designer: Erin Lincoln

(a) BANNER

1. Die-cut large and small flowers from assorted patterned paper and cardstock. Adhere together.
2. Sew buttons onto flowers with twine and tie onto flip flops.
3. Die-cut ovals from cardstock. Adhere.
4. Die-cut letters from patterned paper. Adhere to spell "Congrats".
5. String flip flops along wooden dowel. Tie twine to ends.

(b) FLIP FLOP LABEL

1. Die-cut large and small flowers from felt. Adhere together.
2. Sew buttons onto flowers with twine and tie onto flip flops.
3. Die-cut label from patterned paper. Stamp vintage finds and horizontal lines.
4. Die-cut large and small flowers from felt. Adhere together.
5. Thread buttons onto flowers with twine and adhere to label.

(c) FOOD LABEL

1. Print food name on cardstock and trim.
2. Trim strip of patterned paper and adhere.
3. Die-cut shell and sand dollar from patterned paper and cardstock. Adhere pieces together and adhere to label.
4. Place in label holder.

(d) INVITATION

1. Make card from cardstock.
2. Stamp curved line and starfish on cardstock. Trim and adhere to cardstock rectangle. Mat with cardstock and adhere panel.
3. Stamp you're invited on patterned paper, die-cut into sun, and adhere.
4. Die-cut flip flops from patterned paper and cardstock; adhere.
5. Punch flowers from patterned paper and adhere.

(e) THANK YOU CARD

1. Make card from cardstock. Trim cardstock and patterned paper strips; adhere.
2. Die-cut waves from cardstock and adhere. Stamp sentiment.
3. Die-cut sun and bikini from assorted patterned paper and adhere.
4. Stamp basic button and small button on cardstock, trim, and thread with twine. Adhere.
5. Punch flower from patterned paper and adhere.

(f) JAR

1. Fill jar with sugar scrub.
2. Trim strip of patterned paper and adhere.
3. Print sentiment on cardstock. Stamp circle label and trim.
4. Die-cut flip flops from patterned paper and cardstock; adhere.
5. Die-cut scalloped circle from cardstock. Adhere to circle. Adhere rhinestones and adhere circle panel to jar.
6. Die-cut scalloped circle from cardstock. Adhere to jar lid.
7. Wrap twine and tie bow.

Try This

Serve desserts that carry the theme: starfish shaped cookies, coconut marshmallows, and margaritas, for example.

Homemade Toasted
Coconut Marshmallows

(c) FOOD LABEL

Beach Feet
Sugar Scrub

THANK YOU SO MUCH.

You're

OLD NAVY

OLD NAVY

VINTAGE FINDS

Homemade Toasted
Coconut Marshmallows

His & Hers Wedding Shower

Designer: Kimberly Crawford

ⓐ CHANDELIER

❶ Paint embroidery hoops.
❷ Trim cardstock, round corners, and stamp 2's, hearts, and sentiment. Adhere.
❸ String hoops together with fishing line and hang.

ⓑ FOAM CUP WITH NAME CARD

❶ Stamp hearts around bottom of foam cup.
❷ Trim cardstock, round corners, and stamp 2's, hearts, and sentiment.
❸ Adhere to candy stick.
❹ Fill foam cup with treats or poker chips and insert name card.

ⓒ COASTER

❶ Die-cut large octagon from patterned paper.
❷ Die-cut medium octagon from felt and adhere.

ⓓ GLASS MARKER

❶ Hole-punch poker chip.
❷ Stamp heart on patterned paper, die-cut and emboss into circle, and adhere.
❸ Thread poker chip with twine and tie around glass.

ⓔ PLACEMAT

❶ Make base from felt.
❷ Trim felt, die-cut hearts, and adhere.

ⓕ PLAYING CARD WRAP

❶ Trim strip of cardstock, mat with cardstock, and wrap around cards. Adhere ends.
❷ Stamp sentiment.
❸ Die-cut and emboss small hearts from cardstock and adhere with foam tape.

ⓖ FOOD PICK

❶ Die-cut and emboss large heart from cardstock.
❷ Tape to toothpick.

Designer Tips

• Use real playing cards to create the chandelier and foam cup cards.

• Stamp half the hearts on the foam cup, let it dry, and then stamp the other half to avoid ink smearing.

Try This

Find chocolate coins to use for poker chips or, replace poker with Old Maid, War, Gin, Crazy Eights, or Pounce.

Classy & Elegant Wedding Shower

Designer: Windy Robinson

ⓐ PLACEMAT
❶ Adhere two patterned paper sheets together to make base.
❷ Trim patterned paper strip and adhere.
❸ Die-cut letter from cardstock and adhere to cardstock. Double-mat with patterned paper. Adhere panel.
❹ Adhere rhinestone flourishes.

ⓑ GAME CARD
❶ Print game instructions on cardstock and trim.
❷ Double-mat with patterned paper.

ⓒ PLACE CARD
❶ Make card from cardstock. Cover with patterned paper.
❷ Trim strip of patterned paper and adhere.
❸ Trim cardstock square, mat with patterned paper, and adhere.
❹ Print guest name on cardstock, trim, and mat with patterned paper. Adhere.
❺ Tie ribbon bow and adhere.

ⓓ NAPKIN RING
❶ Trim strip of patterned paper and mat with patterned paper.
❷ Adhere rhinestone and adhere ends to form ring.

ⓔ THANK YOU NOTE
❶ Make card from cardstock. Cover with patterned paper.
❷ Trim patterned paper rectangle, mat with cardstock, and adhere.
❸ Stamp thank you on cardstock, mat with patterned paper, and adhere with foam tape.
❹ Tie bow with ribbon and adhere.
❺ Place cards in box.

ⓕ INIVITATION
❶ Make card from patterned paper. Cover with patterned paper and adhere patterned paper strip.
❷ Print text on cardstock and trim. Mat with patterned paper and adhere.
❸ Tie bow with ribbon and adhere.

ⓖ VOTIVE FAVOR
❶ Trim patterned paper strip and adhere around votive.
❷ Stamp thank you on cardstock, mat with patterned paper, and adhere. Adhere rhinestone and rhinestone flourish.
❸ Make box from patterned paper. Trim strip of patterned paper and adhere.
❹ Stamp thank you on cardstock, trim, and adhere rhinestone. Adhere.
❺ Wrap ribbon and tie bow.
❻ Wrap votive in tulle and set in box.

ⓗ VASE
❶ Die-cut letter from cardstock and adhere to cardstock.
❷ Double-mat with patterned paper.
❸ Hole-punch tag, thread ribbon, and tie around vase.
❹ Adhere rhinestone flourish.

ⓘ WISHES BOX
❶ Cover box with patterned paper strips.
❷ Wrap ribbon and tie bow.
❹ Stamp wishes on cardstock, trim, and adhere rhinestone. Adhere to bow.

ⓙ WISH CARD
❶ Make card from cardstock.
❷ Trim patterned paper and adhere.
❸ Stamp heartfelt wishes.
❹ Trim tulle strip, wrap, and tie bow.

Bonus Ideas

• Instead of a wishes box, consider a recipe box where guests bring new recipes for the bride.

• Use the bride's wedding colors instead of fuchsia and brown.

Designer Tip

Game template can be found on included CD.

Try This

Send wishes cards out with the invitations and ask guests to write a heartfelt wish or word of advice on the card and bring it to the shower. Give the box to the bride as the last gift of the day.

PLEASE JOIN US FOR
A BRIDAL LUNCHEON IN HONOR OF

ANNA LIZ ROSE

SATURDAY, MARCH 1
3:00 IN THE AFTERNOON

THE MARKET RESTAURANT
1234 RIVER STREET
CINCINNATI, OH

HOSTED BY HER MATRON OF HONOR
RSVP TO 123.123.1234

Wishes

Thank You

Thank You

APRIL

Thank You

WEDDING ABCS

Heartfelt Wishes

@

Hydrangea Wedding Shower

Designer: Davinie Fiero

ⓐ POMANDER

1. Punch hydrangeas from cardstock and patterned paper. Layer and attach to foam ball with pins.
2. Repeat, alternating craft pins and brads, until ball is covered.
3. Trim ribbon and pin to top. Tie bow to create handle.

ⓑ SHOWER CONE

1. Trim patterned paper.
2. Fold and adhere to create cone.
3. Punch holes at top, thread ribbon, and wrap around. Tie bow.
4. Punch hydrangeas from cardstock and patterned paper. Fill cone.

ⓒ BANNER

1. Trim large and medium pennants from assorted patterned paper; punch holes.
2. Thread floss through tissue flowers and pennants.

ⓓ NAPKIN RING

1. Trim strip of patterned paper. Adhere end to form ring.
2. Adhere tissue flowers.

ⓔ SEATING CARD

1. Print name and table assignment on patterned paper.
2. Punch into tag.

ⓕ TABLE CARD

1. Make card from patterned paper.
2. Die-cut cardstock to spell "Table" and adhere.
3. Die-cut table numbers from cardstock and adhere.

ⓖ GIFT BOX

1. Make box from patterned paper, following pattern on included disk.
2. Assemble box and adhere hook and loop fastener.
3. Fill box with candy or almonds.
4. Tie on ribbon.

ⓗ INVITATION

1. Make card from cardstock.
2. Trim patterned paper panel and border-punch.
3. Adhere patterned paper square.
4. Border-punch patterned paper strip, adhere ribbon, and adhere to panel.
5. Attach brads.
6. Adhere panel and stitch edges.
7. Die-cut cardstock to spell "Join us" and adhere.

ⓘ THANK YOU CARD

1. Make card from cardstock.
2. Trim patterned paper rectangle and adhere patterned paper strip. Stitch edges.
3. Border-punch patterned paper strip, adhere behind panel, and adhere panel to card.
4. Attach brads.
5. Die-cut cardstock to spell "Thank you" and adhere.

Try This

Arrange the seating cards in alphabetical order so that your guests can easily find their names and corresponding seat assignments.

...thank you

Join Us

Smith
#14

table 14

Rehearsal Dinner

Designer: Anabelle O'Malley

ⓐ GIFT BAG

1. Trim strip of patterned paper; adhere to bag.
2. Adhere ribbon. Border-punch cardstock and patterned paper strips; adhere.
3. Die-cut oval from cardstock and adhere with foam tape. Adhere transparency frame.
4. Adhere chipboard heart with foam tape.
5. Wrap heart with twine, thread charm, and adhere with foam tape.
6. Tie on ribbon. Thread button with twine and tie on.
7. Attach pin.

ⓑ TIN

1. Trim patterned paper strips and adhere around tin.
2. Adhere chipboard heart with foam tape.
3. Thread button and charm with twine and adhere.

ⓒ WATER BOTTLE

1. Trim patterned paper strip and adhere around bottle.
2. Border-punch cardstock strip and adhere.
3. Hole-punch chipboard heart.
4. Thread charm and heart with twine and tie. Adhere.

ⓓ CANDY BAR WRAP

1. Trim patterned paper, wrap candy bar, and adhere ends.
2. Wrap ribbon and adhere.
3. Affix stickers to chipboard heart to spell sentiment and adhere with foam tape.

ⓔ INVITATION

1. Print text on cardstock.
2. Wrap ribbon and tie bow.
3. Mat with patterned paper.
4. Border-punch strip of cardstock and adhere.
5. Adhere chipboard heart with foam tape.
6. Wrap heart with twine, thread charm, and adhere with foam tape.

ⓕ PHOTO ALBUM

1. Trim patterned paper and adhere to album.
2. Wrap ribbon and tie bow.
3. Thread button with twine and tie on. Attach pin.
4. Die-cut oval from cardstock and adhere with foam tape.
5. Affix stickers to transparency flourish to spell "Photos" and adhere.

ⓖ RUNNER

Zigzag-stitch all seams.

1. Trim strips of patterned paper and cardstock; adhere together.

Try This

Have guests who have known the couple for years share a funny or touching anecdote after dinner.

It's a Wedding
Rehearsal Dinner...

In anticipation of our big day,
Please join Anabelle and Fran
for dinner, drinks and fun
immediately following
the rehearsal.

Saturday, February 11.
7:00 PM
Elm Street Grill
Wilmington, DE

RSVP by February 1.

Photos

F and A

Fantasy Baby Shower

Designer: Becky Olsen

ⓐ INVITATION

1. Make invitation from patterned paper.
2. Print text on patterned paper, trim, and hole-punch. Trim tag from patterned paper; punch hole. Tie tag to printed panel with twine.
3. Trim patterned paper frame, wrap twine, and adhere. Stitch three edges to form pocket.
4. Die-cut flower from patterned paper and adhere. Insert printed panel.

ⓑ THANK YOU CARD

1. Make card from cardstock. Cover with patterned paper.
2. Trim image from patterned paper, wrap with twine, and adhere with foam tape.
3. Print "Thank you" on patterned paper, trim, and adhere with foam tape.
4. Die-cut flower from patterned paper and adhere.

ⓒ MINI ALBUM

1. Cover album with patterned paper.
2. Trim flowers from patterned paper and adhere.
3. Border-punch strip of patterned paper and adhere.
4. Die-cut circle and scalloped circle from patterned paper and adhere.
5. Trim fairy from patterned paper and adhere.
6. Wrap journal with twine and tie bow.

ⓓ NAPKIN RING

1. Trim strip of patterned paper and mat with patterned paper. Border-punch.
2. Adhere ends to form ring. Wrap twine and adhere.
3. Trim image from patterned paper and adhere with foam tape.

ⓔ GIFT BOX

1. Make box from patterned paper, following pattern found on CD. Assemble.
2. Trim patterned paper strip and adhere.
3. Wrap twine and tie bow.
4. Trim tag from patterned paper, hole-punch, and thread with twine. Tie on.
5. Die-cut flower from patterned paper and adhere.

ⓕ BANNER

1. Trim pennant from patterned paper. Mat with patterned paper and border-punch.
2. Die-cut circles and scalloped circles from patterned paper. Die-cut circle from patterned paper. Adhere together and adhere to pennants with foam tape.
3. Adhere chipboard letters to spell name.
4. Hole-punch pennants. Tie pennants together with twine.
5. Trim tags from patterned paper, hole-punch, and tie on with twine.

ⓖ CENTERPIECE

1. Trim patterned paper, wrap around foam, and adhere.
2. Trim patterned paper strip, mat with patterned paper, and border punch. Adhere.
3. Trim tag from patterned paper, hole-punch, thread with twine, and wrap around center piece. Tie bow.
4. Die-cut flowers from patterned paper and adhere.
5. Trim fairies from patterned paper, adhere to wire, and insert in foam.

Designer Tip

Make all of the flowers you will need and then a few extras in one sitting if you can. This will make the process go much faster and you can do this while doing other tasks like watching TV, listening to music, or a book on CD.

Try This

Make an extra invitation without the insert and place a photo of the baby in the opening. Frame in a shadow box as a keepsake gift for the new parents after the baby is born.

ⓐ INVITATION

Carnival Baby Shower

Designer: Heidi Van Laar

ⓐ INVITATION

1. Make card from cardstock.
2. Trim patterned paper rectangles and adhere.
3. Trim patterned paper rectangle. Trim patterned paper strip with decorative-edge scissors and adhere behind rectangle. Adhere chipboard corners and adhere panel with foam tape.
4. Stamp party info on popcorn tag insert. Tie twine to popcorn pocket and adhere with foam tape. Place tag insert into pocket.
5. Tie bow with twine and adhere. Adhere chipboard star.
6. Stamp "Baby shower" on journal tag, trim, and adhere with foam tape.

ⓑ THANK YOU CARD

1. Make card from cardstock.
2. Trim patterned paper panel. Adhere patterned paper strip.
3. Wrap twine around card and adhere. Adhere flags.
4. Die-cut label from cardstock and adhere with foam tape.
5. Stamp "Thank you" on cardstock, trim, and adhere with foam tape.
6. Adhere chipboard elephant. Tie bow with twine and adhere. Adhere chipboard star.

ⓒ PLACE CARD

1. Make card from cardstock.
2. Die-cut scalloped border from patterned paper and cardstock. Trim and adhere.
3. Adhere chipboard band member.
4. Stamp name.

ⓓ GAME CARD

1. Trim and score cardstock panel. Round bottom corners.
2. Mat with patterned paper.
3. Stamp "Games" and numbers.
4. Trim ticket from patterned paper; adhere.
5. Adhere chipboard circle and glitter dot.

ⓔ PARTY CRACKER

1. Trim paper towel roll. Wrap with crepe paper and tie ends with twine.
2. Trim patterned paper strip and adhere. Trim strip of patterned paper with decorative-edge scissors, wrap, and adhere.
3. Trim crepe paper with decorative-edge scissors, stitch, and adhere.
4. Assemble and adhere flag and glitter dot.

ⓕ NAPKIN RING

1. Trim strip of patterned paper, mat with cardstock, and trim with decorative-edge scissors.
2. Adhere ends together to form ring.
3. Trim ticket strip from patterned paper and adhere.
4. Trim patterned paper strip, score, and accordion-fold to create rosette. Adhere ends and press flat. Adhere.
5. Adhere chipboard wheel.
6. Trim tickets from patterned paper and adhere. Adhere rhinestone.

ⓖ BANNER

1. Trim pennants from cardstock using pattern on included CD.
2. Adhere ribbon and tie pennants together.
3. Trim pennants from patterned paper and adhere.
4. Trim strips of patterned paper, score, and accordion-fold to create rosettes. Adhere ends and press flat. Adhere.
5. Die-cut circles and scalloped circles from patterned paper. Adhere together and adhere to banner.
6. Paint chipboard letters and adhere to spell "Baby".

ⓗ CUPCAKE TOPPER

1. Trim pennants from patterned paper.
2. Fold pennants over twine and adhere.
3. Trim strips of patterned paper, score, and accordion-fold to create rosettes. Adhere ends and press flat. Adhere.
4. Adhere chipboard wheels and rhinestones.
5. Tie ends of twine to chopsticks and adhere.

Designer Tip

If you embellish only the front side of a banner, it may hang slightly off balance. Try creating counterweights by adding coins or metal discs covered with patterned paper to the backsides.

Try This

Use the numbered game card to list answers to popular shower games like guessing the due date, baby's weight, circumference of mommy-to-be's belly, favorite craving, etc.

Bun in the Oven

Designer: Julie Campbell

ⓐ OVEN

1. Using template found on CD, make oven from patterned paper; assemble.
2. Ink edges and trim transparency sheet. Adhere to inside of oven door.
3. Stamp large flowers and color.
4. Stamp small flowers and sweet baby on cardstock. Trim, ink edges, and color. Adhere.
5. Adhere metal oven mitt.
6. Trim fabric and adhere.
7. Place tart in tin and place in oven.

ⓑ RECIPE CARD

1. Stamp recipe card on cardstock. Trim and ink.
2. Stamp mixing bowl and color.
3. Stamp kitchen sentiment.
4. Spray with shimmer spray.

ⓒ THANK YOU CARD

1. Make card from cardstock. Round corners and ink edges.
2. Trim strip of patterned paper and adhere.
3. Stamp recipe card and oven mitt on patterned paper. Trim and adhere.
4. Stamp oven mitt on cardstock, color, and trim. Adhere with foam tape.
5. Affix stickers to spell "Thank you".

ⓓ INVITATION

1. Make card from cardstock. Round corners.
2. Trim patterned paper strips, round corners, ink edges, and adhere together.
3. Stamp bun sentiment.
4. Trim patterned paper strip and adhere.
5. Wrap thread, tie bow, and adhere panel.
6. Stamp oven on patterned paper, trim, and color.
7. Stamp muffin and oven on cardstock. Color, trim, and adhere. Paper-piece and adhere with foam tape.

ⓔ ENVELOPE

1. Die-cut patterned paper and adhere to inside of envelope.
2. Stamp "It's a shower" on front.
3. Stamp muffin on cardstock. Color, trim, and adhere.

ⓕ MEASURING SPOON FAVOR

1. Print sentiment on cardstock.
2. Stamp label and trim.
3. Spray with shimmer spray and punch slot.
4. Thread with fabric strip and tie to measuring spoons.

ⓖ CINNAMON BUN FAVOR

1. Stamp sentiment on strip of patterned paper.
2. Border-punch patterned paper and adhere.
3. Place tart in tin and place in cellophane bag.
4. Adhere panel to bag and staple closed.

See detailed image of favor on p. 283

Designer Tip

Remove the top of your shimmer spray and allow ink to drop onto your projects to give them an aged appearance.

Try This

Serve warm, made-from-scratch cinnamon rolls to guests instead of traditional cake, or have the guests write down tips or advice on recipe cards for the new mother-to-be.

ⓓ there's a bun in the oven!

ⓔ ...s a shower 🧁

ⓒ thank you

ⓑ from the kitchen of:

from the kitchen of:

from the kitchen of:

bun in the oven

ⓐ Sweet BABY

ⓖ

○ love beyond measure ♡

Fun & Cute Baby Shower

Designer: Kalyn Kepner

ⓐ SODA WRAP

1. Trim cardstock strip.
2. Trim patterned paper with decorative-edge scissors and adhere.
3. Die-cut label from patterned paper and adhere with foam tape.
4. Print "Enjoy" on die cut ticket and adhere with foam tape.

ⓑ CUPCAKE TOPPER

1. Die-cut label from cardstock and ink edges.
2. Trim cardstock circle with decorative-edge scissors, stitch, and adhere.
3. Adhere chipboard piece.
4. Adhere toothpick.

ⓒ INVITATION

1. Make card from cardstock. Cover with patterned paper.
2. Trim cardstock, ink edges, and print sentiment. Adhere and stitch edges.
3. Trim cardstock strip; adhere. Trim patterned paper strip with decorative edge scissors; adhere. Zigzag-stitch.
4. Adhere chipboard umbrella.
5. Trim rain drops from patterned paper and adhere.

ⓓ THANK YOU CARD

1. Make card from cardstock.
2. Print "Thank you" on cardstock, trim, and adhere.
3. Trim patterned paper, mat with patterned paper, and trim edges with decorative-edge scissors.
4. Trim patterned paper strip, adhere behind panel, and adhere panel to card.
5. Adhere chipboard pieces.

ⓔ GIFT BOX

1. Make box from cardstock.
2. Trim patterned paper strips with decorative-edge scissors and adhere.
3. Trim patterned paper and cardstock strips and adhere.
4. Adhere chipboard bees.

ⓕ TREAT BAG TOPPER

1. Die-cut label from patterned paper and fold in half; ink edges.
2. Trim circles from cardstock with decorative-edge scissors; adhere.
3. Thread button with floss and adhere.

ⓖ BANNER

1. Trim pennants from cardstock.
2. Trim patterned paper and adhere.
3. Trim cardstock using decorative-edge scissors; adhere.
4. Trim cardstock and fold to make rosettes, ink edges, and adhere.
5. Punch circles from patterned paper and adhere.
6. Punch circles from patterned paper, mat with patterned paper, and trim edges with decorative-edge scissors. Adhere with foam tape.
7. Affix stickers to spell "Baby".
8. Adhere banner to ribbon.

Sweet Baby Girl

Designer: Layle Koncar

ⓐ INVITATION

1. Trim patterned paper.
2. Trim strip of patterned paper and adhere to form pocket; ink edges.
3. Border-punch strip of patterned paper and adhere.
4. Adhere pearl strips. Adhere trim.
5. Adhere wooden button and pearl.
6. Print text on patterned paper, ink edges, and mat with patterned paper. Insert in pocket.

ⓑ THANK YOU NOTE

1. Make card from patterned paper.
2. Stamp thank you on patterned paper, trim, and ink edges. Adhere.
3. Trim patterned paper rectangle, ink edges, and adhere.
4. Border-punch strip of patterned paper and adhere.
5. Adhere trim and pearl strips.

ⓒ NOTEBOOK

1. Trim fabric and adhere.
2. Trim tag from patterned paper, ink edges, and adhere.
3. Adhere trim and pearl strips.
4. Adhere button and pearl.

ⓓ CENTERPIECE

1. Trim strip of patterned paper and adhere to bucket.
2. Adhere strips of trim.
3. Fill bucket with packing peanuts and cover with gift shred.
4. Affix stickers to lollipop sticks, mat back with scrap paper, and ink edges. Adhere rose. Insert sticks into bucket.
5. Punch two scalloped circles from patterned paper and adhere to lollipop stick. Ink edges, adhere button, and adhere pearl. Insert stick into bucket.

ⓔ NAME TAG

1. Trim strip of crepe paper, bunch, and adhere.
2. Punch scalloped circle from patterned paper; adhere.
3. Print guest name on patterned paper, trim, and ink edges. Attach with stick pin.
4. Apply glitter to edges.

ⓕ NAPKIN RING

1. Trim patterned paper strip. Adhere ends together.
2. Wrap with trim and adhere.
3. Tie ribbon to safety pin and attach to trim.
4. Attach pacifier charm to safety pin.

ⓖ CUPCAKE WRAPPER

1. Trim patterned paper strip with decorative-edge scissors; ink edges.
2. Adhere ends together.

◯ CUPCAKE TOPPER

1. Punch two scalloped circles from patterned paper.
2. Adhere to lollipop stick with foam tape.
3. Trim rose from trim and adhere.
4. Apply glitter glue to edges.

ⓘ GOODY BAG

1. Trim patterned paper strip.
2. Border punch bottom edge.
3. Fill cellophane bag with candies, adhere patterned paper strip, and staple shut.
4. Adhere brooch and pearl.

Designer Tip

Rather than using stickers for the centerpiece, you can create several name tag pinwheels using different colors and coordinating crepe paper.

Sweet Content

thank you

A Baby Shower!

Savor
THESE MOMENTS

Susan

Modern Baby Boy Shower

Designer: Maile Belles

(a) PLACE CARD

1. Make card from patterned paper.
2. Stamp leaves and leaf outlines on cardstock.
3. Trim and adhere.
4. Thread button with floss and adhere.

(b) CUPCAKE TOPPER

1. Stamp star and ball tags on cardstock and die-cut.
2. Stamp letters to spell "Boy". Stamp sweet baby.
3. Pierce holes through straw tops.
4. Thread floss through tags and straws. Tie ends.

(c) FAVOR BOX

1. Die-cut box from cardstock.
2. Score, fold, and assemble box. Adhere.
3. Stamp leaves and leaf outlines on cardstock. Trim and adhere.
4. Thread button with floss and adhere.
5. Wrap ribbon and tie bow.

(d) INVITATION

1. Make card from cardstock. Adhere cardstock.
2. Stamp leaves and leaf outlines on cardstock. Trim and adhere.
3. Trim strip of cardstock and adhere.
4. Stamp stars, ball, and sentiments on cardstock; die-cut.
5. Thread tags and button with floss; adhere button.
6. Adhere tags with foam tape.

(e) THANK YOU CARD

1. Make card from cardstock. Adhere cardstock.
2. Stamp leaves and leaf outlines on cardstock. Trim and adhere. Adhere cardstock strip.
3. Stamp star tag and thank you on cardstock; die-cut.
4. Thread tag and buttons with floss and adhere.

(f) NAPKIN WRAPS

1. Trim cardstock strip. Stamp leaves and leaf outlines on cardstock. Trim and adhere.
2. Wrap strip around napkin and adhere ends.
3. Thread button with twine and adhere.

(g) BANNER PENNANT

1. Die-cut large banner from cardstock.
2. Die-cut small banner from cardstock and adhere. Stamp letter.
3. Stamp leaves and leaf outlines on cardstock, trim, and adhere.
4. Loop ribbon and adhere.
5. Thread button with floss and adhere.

Designer Tips

- Since the banner pennants are not attached to each other, they can be attached to a wall in an arch, straight, horizontal, or vertical arrangement.

- The banner cake topper can be placed on top of a cake or into two cupcakes.

- The "patterned paper" for this ensemble was stamped by hand. If hand stamping your own coordinating pattern, start by stamping a full sheet. Then you can divide and trim the sheet into the pieces needed for project assembly.

Try This

Hand stamping your own patterned paper allows you to create a party ensemble in any color combination you choose!

Sacred Celebration

Designer: Beth Opel

(a) FRAME

1. Adhere patterned paper to canvas.
2. Adhere ribbon.
3. Affix stickers to spell sentiment.
4. Adhere flowers. Punch leaves from cardstock and adhere.
5. Adhere pearls.
6. Place panel in frame.

(b) BOX

1. Make box bottom from cardstock and box lid from patterned paper.
2. Adhere trim to lid border.
3. Tie on ribbon.
4. Adhere flowers. Punch leaves from cardstock and adhere.
5. Print sentiment on label sticker and adhere with foam tape.
6. Adhere pearls.

(c) CARD

1. Make card from patterned paper.
2. Trim and adhere patterned paper.
3. Adhere ribbon.
4. Print sentiment on label sticker and adhere with foam tape.
5. Adhere flowers. Punch leaves from cardstock and adhere.
6. Adhere pearls.

(d) BOOKMARK

1. Print verse on cardstock.
2. Trim two book marks from cardstock; round corners.
3. Sandwich velvet ribbon between bookmarks and adhere together.
4. Trim patterned paper, round corners, and adhere.
5. Adhere ribbon and trim.
6. Affix cross sticker to ribbon and adhere pearl.

(e) BANNER

1. Trim ribbon and tie knot at each end.
2. Hole-punch letters and attach to ribbon with brads to spell sentiment.
3. Attach safety pins through knots.

(f) CUPCAKE WRAPS

1. Trim strip of cardstock. Cover with patterned paper.
2. Adhere trim.
3. Staple ends together.
4. Affix cross sticker and adhere pearl.

Designer Tips

- Print label sentiment on plain paper first. Then, affix label directly over the sentiment and run it through the printer again.

- Don't have any canvas board? Use cardboard instead!

- Bible verse from Joshua 1:9 on the bookmark can be found on included CD.

GOD BE WITH YOU

I am a CHILD of GOD

God's richest blessings to you

On this Sacred Day

DEUTERONOMY 33:26

Joshua

15 Years & Counting

Designer: Kalyn Kepner

ⓐ INVITATION

❶ Make invitation from cardstock.
❷ Stamp you're invited and adhere pattered paper square. *Note: Ink edges of pattered paper before adhering.*
❸ Affix flower stickers.

ⓑ GUEST BOOK

❶ Cut chipboard and patterned paper to finished size.
❷ Mat patterned paper rectangle with patterned paper. Stitch border and adhere to chipboard rectangle.
❸ Adhere round label with foam tape.
❹ Trim flowers from patterned paper. Curl petals and adhere.
❺ Stamp flourishes and happy anniversary on cardstock. Trim into banner, ink edges, and adhere with foam tape.
❻ Adhere pearls.
❼ Hole-punch chipboard and patterned paper. Tie together with ribbon.

ⓒ BOTTLE WRAP

❶ Trim patterned paper rectangles.
❷ Border-punch patterned paper strips; adhere.
❸ Adhere panel around bottle.

ⓓ CUPCAKE TOPPER

❶ Die-cut square label from patterned paper.
❷ Accordion-fold patterned paper strip; adhere into circle. Adhere to die-cut panel.
❸ Print "15" on cardstock, die-cut into medium scalloped circle, ink edges, and adhere.
❹ Adhere panel to toothpick.

ⓔ APPETIZER PICK

❶ Stamp flourishes and happy anniversary on cardstock strip.
❷ Adhere around toothpick, trim into flag, and ink edges.
❸ Trim flower from patterned paper; adhere.

ⓕ CAKE TOPPER

❶ Paint flag; let dry.
❷ Adhere patterned paper to flag; ink edges.
❸ Trim flower from patterned paper; adhere with foam tape. Affix border sticker.
❹ Print "15" on cardstock, die-cut into rectangle label, ink edges, and adhere.
❺ Affix flower sticker.

ⓖ BANNER

❶ Trim pennants from cardstock.
❷ Trim patterned paper slightly smaller than pennants. Border-punch patterned paper strips; adhere. Adhere panels to cardstock.
❸ Die-cut square labels from patterned paper; ink edges.
❹ Trim flowers from patterned paper; adhere to labels. Print "15" on cardstock, trim, and adhere to labels with foam tape.
❺ Die-cut small scalloped circles from patterned paper. Adhere flowers and adhere to labels.
❻ Adhere labels to pennants with foam tape.
❼ Adhere pennants to ribbon.

ⓗ FRAME

❶ Adhere patterned paper to frame; ink edges.
❷ Trim patterned paper strips with decorative-edge scissors; adhere.
❸ Trim and affix flowering vines sticker. Adhere bird stamp with foam tape; adhere flower.
❹ Stamp flourishes and sentiment on cardstock, trim, ink edges, and adhere with foam tape.

ⓘ BAG TOPPER

❶ Punch scalloped square from patterned paper. Ink edges and fold.
❷ Die-cut small scalloped circle from patterned paper; adhere. Adhere flower.

Designer Tip

Save money by creating custom embellishments with your favorite die cuts, punches, and decorative-edge scissors.

Stunningly Silver

Designer: Lisa Johnson

ⓐ INVITATION

❶ Make invitation from cardstock.

❷ Trim patterned paper slightly smaller than card front, adhere ribbon, and adhere to card.

❸ Stamp sentiment on cardstock strip; adhere.

❹ Die-cut "25" from patterned paper; adhere with foam tape.

❺ Adhere tulle fan. Curl butterfly die cuts, adhere rhinestones, and adhere to card.

ⓑ BOTTLE WRAP

❶ Trim patterned paper to finished size.

❷ Stamp happy anniversary on cardstock, circle-punch, adhere rhinestones, and adhere to panel.

❸ Adhere ribbon and tulle.

❹ Die-cut tag from cardstock, stamp "25", adhere rhinestone, and adhere.

❺ Curl butterfly die cut, adhere rhinestone, and adhere.

❻ Adhere panel around bottle.

ⓒ THANK YOU CARD & ENVELOPE

❶ Make card from cardstock.

❷ Die-cut label from cardstock, stamp thank you, and adhere rhinestone. Adhere to card.

❸ Die-cut envelope from patterned paper; assemble.

❹ Curl butterfly die cut, adhere rhinestone, and adhere to envelope.

ⓓ CUPCAKE TOPPER

❶ Adhere butterfly die cuts to either side of candy stick.

❷ Adhere rhinestones and tie on tulle.

ⓔ FAVOR CAN

❶ Adhere patterned paper around can.

❷ Stamp happy anniversary on cardstock, circle-punch, adhere rhinestones, and adhere to can.

❸ Tie on ribbon and tulle.

❹ Curl butterfly die cut, adhere rhinestone, and adhere.

ⓕ TOPIARY CENTERPIECE

❶ Paint clay pot, wood dowel, and foam ball; let dry.

❷ Insert dowel into foam ball and wrap with tulle.

❸ Curl butterfly die cuts, adhere rhinestones, and adhere.

❹ Tie on ribbon. Adhere button and rhinestone.

❺ Die-cut "25" from patterned paper; adhere to pot with foam tape.

❻ Insert embellished ball and dowel inside pot. *Note: Glue foam to the bottom of the pot before inserting dowel.*

Try This

- Create an extra elegant environment by inviting your guests to wear white and silver to the party.

- Many zoos rent out spaces for parties. Match your decor to your surroundings by celebrating your 25th anniversary in the butterfly house at your local zoo.

Fabulous 50th

Designer: Andrea Bowden, courtesy of Stampin' Up!

ⓐ INVITATION

❶ Create project in software.
❷ Add digital cardstock. *Note: Add cardstock for base and photo mats.*
❸ Add digital photo text template, photos, and masking tape. Add drop shadows behind photo mats.
❹ Add digital doily, twine, and bow.
❺ Type sentiment and print invitation on cardstock.
❻ Flower-punch cardstock, stitch with thread, and adhere.

ⓑ JOURNAL

❶ Create project in software.
❷ Add digital cardstock.
❸ Add digital photo text template, doilies, and masking tape. *Note: Change colors and opacity of masking tape strips.*
❹ Type sentiment and add drop shadows behind masking tape.
❺ Print design on cardstock; adhere to journal.
❻ Tie on twine. Flower-punch cardstock, stitch on button with thread, and attach to twine with clothespin.

ⓒ TABLE CARD

❶ Create project in software.
❷ Add digital cardstock.
❸ Add digital photo text template, doily, and masking tape. *Note: Change color and opacity of masking tape strip.*
❹ Type sentiment and print on cardstock.
❺ Trim top of doily from cardstock; fold sides.
❻ Flower-punch cardstock, stitch with thread, and adhere.

ⓓ BANNER

❶ Create project in software.
❷ Create individual pennants and add digital cardstock. *Note: Add cardstock for pennants and photo mats.*
❸ Add digital photo text templates, photos, and masking tape.
❹ Add drop shadows behind photo mats.
❺ Type captions and print pennants on cardstock. *Note: Create one pennant without a photo and caption before printing.*
❻ Print dollies on cardstock; trim.
❼ Adhere pennants and doilies to twine. Flower-punch cardstock and adhere. *Note: Thread one punched flower with thread before adhering.*
❽ Attach clothespins and adhere chipboard numbers.

ⓔ CUPCAKE TOPPER

❶ Create project in software.
❷ Fill digital punches with patterned paper and cardstock; print on cardstock.
❸ Print doilies on cardstock.
❹ Trim flags and adhere to twine and toothpicks.
❺ Trim doilies and adhere with foam tape.

ⓕ FAVOR BOXES

❶ Repeat Steps 1-3 from Cupcake Topper.
❷ Tie twine around small box. Trim flags and small doily; adhere.
❸ Tie twine around large box. Trim large doily, stitch on button with twine, and adhere.

Try This

Before the party, ask 50 family members and friends for 50 brief memories and compile them for a memorable gift.

Beautiful Butterflies

Designer: Alicia Thelin

ⓐ INVITATION

1. Die-cut bracketed border from cardstock. Trim cardstock rectangle to finished size, round top corners, and stitch to die cut panel to create pocket.
2. Circle-punch patterned paper; adhere.
3. Die-cut leafy branch from cardstock; adhere.
4. Die-cut butterflies from cardstock, stamp houndstooth butterflies, and staple together. Adhere.
5. Tie on string.
6. Stamp invitation details on cardstock, mat with cardstock, and slot-punch.
7. Thread and staple patterned paper strip through slot. Insert inside pocket.

ⓑ FAVOR BOX

1. Die-cut box from cardstock; assemble.
2. Hole-punch sides and tie on string and ribbon.
3. Circle-punch cardstock, stamp sentiment, and attach to box with brads.
4. Die-cut butterflies from cardstock, staple together, and adhere.

ⓒ FOOD PICK

1. Circle-punch patterned paper.
2. Die-cut leafy branches from cardstock, adhere to circle, and trim.
3. Emboss cardstock, die-cut butterfly, and attach binder clip. Adhere to panel with foam tape.
4. Punch scalloped circle from cardstock; adhere behind panel.
5. Adhere skewer between circles.

ⓓ GARLAND

1. Die-cut butterflies from patterned paper.
2. Stitch to twine.

ⓔ THANKS CARD

1. Make card from cardstock; die-cut butterfly.
2. Tie on ribbon and adhere pearl.
3. Die-cut leafy branch from cardstock. Place negative over cardstock and ink.
4. Remove die-cut negative, stamp thanks, and trim into rectangle. Adhere inside card.
5. Punch scalloped circles from patterned paper; adhere to back and inside front flap of card.

Designer Tip

Make your garland smaller and place it on the top layers of a cake for a fun paper-crafted touch.

Try This

This ensemble could easily be used for a bridal shower, baby shower, or Mother's Day brunch.

It's Your Day

Designer: Jennifer McGuire

ⓐ INVITATION

1. Emboss note card. Circle-punch corners.
2. Print text on cardstock, trim, mat with patterned paper, and trim. Adhere.
3. Die-cut circle and star from patterned paper; adhere.
4. Print text on cardstock. Circle-punch and adhere with foam tape.
5. Punch stars from patterned paper; adhere. Adhere rhinestones.

ⓑ BOTTLE WRAP

1. Trim patterned paper to finished size. Adhere patterned paper strips.
2. Print text on cardstock. Circle-punch and adhere with foam tape.
3. Punch stars from patterned paper; adhere. Adhere rhinestones.
4. Adhere panel around bottle.

ⓒ CUPCAKE TOPPER

1. Die-cut circle and star from patterned paper; adhere.
2. Print text on cardstock; circle-punch. Adhere to die cuts with foam tape.
3. Adhere panel to toothpick.

ⓓ HAT

1. Stamp stars on patterned paper; draw dots with marker.
2. Adhere patterned paper strip and adhere to create hat.
3. Print text on cardstock. Circle-punch and adhere with foam tape.
4. Punch stars from patterned paper; adhere. Adhere rhinestones.

ⓔ CROWN

1. Trim crown from patterned paper. Adhere patterned paper strips.
2. Die-cut circle and star from patterned paper; adhere.
3. Print text on cardstock. Circle-punch and adhere with foam tape.
4. Punch stars from patterned paper; adhere. Adhere rhinestones.
5. Adhere ends together to create crown.

Designer Tip

Get your kids involved. Have your child write a sentiment and then scan it into your computer for a personal touch.

Try This

Some people are so cool, they deserve a party just because. Throw a fun party for someone who deserves to be celebrated no matter the time of year.

e · I AM UNCLE MIKE AND I RULE

b · Uncle Mike RULES

d · MY Uncle Mike ROCKS

c · Uncle Mike ROCKS · Uncle Mike RULES · Uncle Mike IS #1!

a · YOU'RE INVITED TO Uncle Mike DAY!

Le Jardin

Designer: Vanessa Menhorn

ⓐ PLACE CARD

1. Make card from patterned paper.
2. Border-punch edge, stamp text, and ink edges.
3. Print name on patterned paper, die-cut into butterfly, and ink edges.
4. Adhere butterfly to card with foam tape. Insert stick pin.

ⓑ FAVOR BAG

1. Border-punch patterned paper strip; adhere to bag.
2. Adhere patterned paper strip; stamp le jardin.
3. Butterfly-punch patterned paper, ink edges, and adhere.
4. Print sentiment on cardstock, die-cut into tag, and ink edges. Die-cut hole reinforcer from patterned paper; adhere.
5. Tie tag to bag with twine.

ⓒ LUMINARY

1. Trim flowers from patterned paper; adhere to vellum.
2. Adhere vellum together to create cylinder.

ⓓ NAPKIN RING

1. Cut patterned paper strip to 6½" x 1¾"; ink edges.
2. Border-punch patterned paper strip; adhere. Adhere together to create ring.
3. Die-cut butterflies from vellum and patterned paper. Ink edges of vellum butterfly and adhere together.
4. Thread button with floss; adhere to butterfly. Adhere to ring.

ⓔ FOOD PICK

1. Die-cut butterflies from patterned paper; ink edges.
2. Punch butterflies from patterned paper; adhere.
3. Adhere butterflies around skewer.
4. Adhere flower.

ⓕ VASE CENTERPIECE

1. Trim and score patterned paper. Adhere to create vase.
2. Border-punch and score patterned paper strip; adhere.
3. Die-cut and punch butterflies from patterned paper. Adhere together, ink edges, and adhere to vase with foam tape.
4. Insert stick pin.

Try This

- Add to your party's ambience by embellishing clear mason jars with coordinating butterflies and twine. Add sand and votives for delicate light.

- Punch butterflies from your scrap paper and scatter them on the table as confetti.

le jardin

Please take a seed...

Susan

Jennifer

Kelly

Welcoming Housewarming

Designer: Alicia Thelin

ⓐ INVITATION

1. Make tri-fold card from cardstock.
2. Stamp Ornate Blossom and you're invited on cardstock rectangle. Ticket corner-punch and adhere with foam tape.
3. Border-punch cardstock strip; adhere.
4. Attach brads.

ⓑ FRIEND CARD

1. Make card from cardstock.
2. Emboss cardstock rectangle; adhere.
3. Tie on ribbon and twine; attach staples.
4. Stamp sentiment on cardstock twice. Trim flower, color with markers, adhere glitter, and adhere to sentiment with foam tape.
5. Trim image and mat with cork. Adhere to card with foam tape.

ⓒ BANNER

1. Punch circles and scalloped circles from cardstock. Adhere together.
2. Die-cut "Welcome" from cardstock.
3. Adhere letters to circles. Adhere twine bows.
4. Adhere pieces to wire.

ⓓ MAGNET

1. Print contact information on cardstock.
2. Stamp vine on panel, emboss, and trim.
3. Round bottom corner, mat with cork, and attach staple. Round bottom corner.
4. Adhere ribbon and magnet behind panel.

ⓔ FAVOR BOX

1. Die-cut box from cardstock; assemble.
2. Border-punch cardstock strip, adhere, and attach brads.
3. Stamp poppy and welcome on cardstock, tag-punch, and tie to cardstock strip.

ⓕ PLATE DECOR

1. Fold crepe paper multiple times, trim flowers, and adhere together at base.
2. Ball-up crepe paper and adhere to center of flowers.
3. Ink petals and center, adhere glitter, and let dry.
4. Thread twine through flower base and tie to tiered plate.
5. Tie on ribbon.

Designer Tip

Put a small note pad and pen, blank recipe cards, or even seed packets in the favor boxes.

Moustache Welcome Home

Designer: Becky Olsen

ⓐ INVITATION

1. Make invitation from patterned paper.
2. Print text on patterned paper, mat with cardstock, and adhere.
3. Mat patterned paper strip with cardstock. Fold around card and adhere in back to create band.
4. Apply rub-on to cardstock, trim, and adhere with foam tape.

ⓑ PLACE CARD

1. Make card from cardstock.
2. Print name on patterned paper, trim slightly smaller than card, and adhere.
3. Apply rub-on to cardstock, trim, and adhere.

ⓒ FOOD PICK

1. Print text on patterned paper; trim.
2. Mat panel with patterned paper and cardstock.
3. Adhere toothpick.
4. Apply rub-on to cardstock, trim, and adhere with foam tape.

ⓓ NAPKIN RING

1. Trim cardstock to 5½" x 2". Adhere patterned paper strip.
2. Staple together to create ring.
3. Apply rub-on to cardstock, trim, and adhere with foam tape.

ⓔ FAVOR BAG

1. Make bag from cardstock. Apply rub-ons and assemble.
2. Fold and trim cardstock to fit top of bag. Adhere slightly smaller patterned paper rectangle.
3. Apply rub-on to cardstock, trim, and adhere.

ⓕ SHADOW BOX

1. Adhere patterned paper to shadow box. Shadow box pattern found on CD.
2. Insert photo.

ⓖ BANNER

1. Die-cut labels from cardstock and patterned paper; adhere together. *Note: Adhere smallest labels with foam tape.*
2. Affix stickers to spell "Welcome home".
3. Attach eyelets and tie together with twine.

ⓗ MOUSTACHE PICK

1. Apply rub-on to cardstock, trim, and adhere to skewer.

Try This

Invite guests to pose for pictures with the moustache sticks for a fun activity.

We are thrilled to
Welcome Tyler home from
his world travels,
and would love for you
to join us in the
celebrating.

We will be enjoying
cuisine from around the
world on Sunday the 27th

Egg "Fu Manchu" Rolls

"Handlebar" Hotdogs

Tyler

Chad

Homey Housewarming

Designer: Julia Stainton

ⓐ INVITATION

1. Make card from cardstock.
2. Cut patterned paper square; sand edges. Mat with patterned paper; sand edges, staple, and adhere to card.
3. Adhere ticket. Make "Please come" label and affix.
4. Cover chipboard house with patterned paper; sand edges and adhere. Adhere number circle.

ⓑ FRAME

1. Cover frame with patterned paper; sand edges.
2. Affix stickers to spell "Home".

ⓒ BANNER

1. Cut cardboard squares.
2. Cut slightly smaller patterned paper squares. Cut chipboard squares, adhere to patterned paper squares, and staple. Adhere to cardboard squares.
3. Affix stickers to spell "Welcome".
4. Cut triangle from patterned paper, adhere to chipboard, trim, and adhere to one panel. Attach staples.
5. Punch holes in panels and string on twine to form banner.

ⓓ FOOD PICK

1. Die-cut rosette from patterned paper; assemble.
2. Cut felt circle; adhere. Thread button with twine and adhere. Adhere house circle.
3. Adhere rosette to skewer.

ⓔ CANDLE

1. Cut patterned paper strip, mat with patterned paper, wrap around candle, and adhere ends.
2. Affix numbers. Tie on twine.

ⓕ WREATH

1. Cover wreath with tape.
2. Cut patterned paper to fit acrylic house page, trim door, and adhere. Adhere to wreath.
3. String pennants on twine; adhere ends to wreath.
4. Die-cut rosette from patterned paper; assemble. Thread button with twine and adhere to rosette. Adhere rosette to wreath.

Try This

Keep ensemble details simple to make it doable after a busy moving experience.

Bonus Idea

With a few little adjustments, this ensemble would also work for a Welcome Home party.

Military Homecoming

Designer: Latisha Yoast

ⓐ INVITATION

1. Die-cut labels from patterned paper. Adhere tops together to create card.
2. Print text on cardstock, die-cut into label, and tie on twine. Adhere to card with foam tape.
3. Affix star stickers.

ⓑ ALBUM

1. Die-cut labels from patterned paper, cardstock, and chipboard.
2. Print "Deployment pictures" on cardstock die cut, trim, and adhere to patterned paper die cut.
3. Bind labels together with binding comb.
4. Adhere patterned paper strip and affix sticker.

ⓒ GUESTS LIST

1. Die-cut labels from patterned paper and cardstock; adhere together.
2. Adhere twill.
3. Print "Guests" on cardstock, die-cut into label, and adhere with foam tape.
4. Affix sticker.

ⓓ TISSUES WRAP FAVOR

1. Adhere twill around tissues.
2. Print "Tissues" on cardstock, die-cut into label, and adhere.
3. Affix sticker.

ⓔ TREAT CAN

1. Adhere patterned paper strip around can.
2. Print sentiment on cardstock, die-cut into label, and adhere.
3. Affix sticker.

ⓕ BANNER

1. Die-cut labels from patterned paper; adhere together with foam tape.
2. Die-cut circles from patterned paper, ink edges, and adhere with foam tape.
3. Affix alphabet stickers to spell "Hero".
4. Hole-punch panels and tie on twill.

ⓖ FOOD PICK

1. Print text on cardstock, die-cut into pennant, and adhere to skewer.

Designer Tip

Buy a bunch of small American flags on sticks to use for decoration and let guests take one home in remembrance of the hero's return.

(f)

H E R O

(b) DEPLOYMENT PICTURES

(c)

FREEDOM FRIES

GUESTS

FIRST KISS MINTS (e)

HOT DOGS (g)

PLEASE JOIN US FOR A HOMECOMING PARTY

TISSUES

(a)

(d)

It's Derby Time!

Designer: Beth Opel

ⓐ INVITATION

1. Print text on cardstock; trim and mat with cardstock.
2. Print photo on photo paper; trim and adhere.
3. Adhere ribbon and flowers.

ⓑ HORSESHOE

1. Cut horseshoe from cardboard, following pattern found on CD.
2. Adhere cardstock and flowers.

ⓒ FOOD PICKS

1. Cut hats from cardstock, following patterns found on CD.
2. Adhere ribbon, flowers, pearls, felt, and rhinestones.
3. Adhere to toothpicks.

ⓓ BANNER

1. Cut rectangles from cardboard; adhere cardstock.
2. Trim diamonds and stripes from cardstock; adhere.
3. Hole-punch panels; thread on ribbon.

ⓔ GIFT BAGS

1. Trim and adhere transparency sheet to bag.
2. Circle-punch cardstock. Score and fold cardstock strip; adhere ends together. Flatten pinwheel and adhere circles to both sides.
3. Adhere ribbon and adhere piece to bag.
4. Affix stickers to spell sentiments and adhere flowers.
5. Insert tissue paper.
6. Repeat for remaining bags.

Designer Tip

Invitation wording can be found on included CD.

Try This

Invite your guests to wear their finest Kentucky Derby attire including hats, spring dresses, and suits.

d

e

place

win

show

b

a

IT'S
*Kentucky
Derby*
TIME!

JOIN US: Saturday, May 5th
5 o'clock in the afternoon
The Cove Clubhouse

our most fabulous hat and cheer on
orite in the 138th Run for the Roses!

c

Time to Tailgate

Designer: Beth Opel

ⓐ FOAM FINGER

❶ Affix stickers to finger to spell "Let's go".
❷ Cut felt into letters to spell "Blue". Adhere.
❸ Affix football.

ⓑ BOTTLE TAG

❶ Print school initials on cardstock; circle-punch.
❷ Hole-punch and tie on elastic.

ⓒ FOOD PICK

❶ Cut fence in half.
❷ Affix "D" sticker to cardstock; trim and adhere to fence with foam tape.

ⓓ FAVOR BOX

❶ Trim and adhere cardstock strips to box.
❷ Affix football.

ⓔ TABLE RUNNER

❶ Adhere felt sheets together. Adhere cardstock strips to seams. *Note: Adhere additional strip to back of each seam for support.*
❷ Affix numbers; cut triangles from stickers and affix.

ⓕ BANNER

❶ Cut pennants from felt.
❷ Cut initials from felt and adhere.
❸ Print school names on cardstock; trim and adhere.
❹ Trim felt strips; loop each over pennant and staple.
❺ Thread ribbon through loops.
❻ Repeat for second banner.

Try This

Serve traditional tailgate food like hamburgers and hot dogs, and encourage your guests to wear t-shirts and jerseys proclaiming their team allegiance.

Movie Night Magic

Designer: Cristina Kowalczyk

ⓐ INVITATION
1. Print text on cardstock; fold into card.
2. Adhere cardstock and patterned paper strips.

ⓑ BOTTLE WRAP
1. Mat patterned paper strip with cardstock.
2. Print "Root beer" on cardstock, trim, and adhere to panel.
3. Adhere around bottle.

ⓒ FAVOR BOX
1. Trim box from patterned paper, following pattern found on CD. Assemble.
2. Print "Popcorn" on cardstock; trim. Mat with cardstock and adhere to box.

ⓓ CANDY CADDY
1. Trim caddy from cardstock, following pattern found on CD. Assemble.
2. Adhere patterned paper rectangle.
3. Print "Candy" on cardstock, trim, and adhere.

ⓔ FOOD PICK
1. Die-cut stars from cardstock; adhere together.
2. Print text on cardstock, trim, and adhere.
3. Adhere piece to skewer.

ⓕ CENTERPIECE
1. Place foam blocks inside tin. Trim tissue paper and adhere.
2. Print "Movie night" on cardstock, trim, and adhere to tin.
3. Die-cut stars from cardstock; adhere together. Adhere to wood skewers and insert in foam.

Designer Tips

- Heat-set your printed cardstock to avoid the text from smearing.

- Place wax paper inside your popcorn boxes before filling to keep them grease-free.

- Invite and food label wording can be found on included CD.

Try This

Like the popular "stay-cation", paper crafting your movie night is a great way to make it extra special all while staying in the comfort of your own home (and saving money).

MOVIE NIGHT

POPCORN

MILK DUDS

JUNIOR MINTS

CANDY

ROOT BEER

You're invited to

MOVIE NIGHT

at the Kowalczyk Theater
(a.k.a. our house)

Saturday, November 12
7:30 p.m.

Bakin' Up Some Cupcakes

Designer: Erin Lincoln

ⓐ INVITATION

1. Make card from cardstock; adhere patterned paper panels.
2. Die-cut circle, scalloped circle, and banner from patterned paper. Adhere circles.
3. Stamp sentiment on banner, adhere cardstock behind openings, and adhere to card. Adhere rhinestones.
4. Die-cut cupcake and rickrack border from patterned paper and cardstock; adhere.
5. Thread button with twine; adhere.

ⓑ FROSTING WRAP

1. Adhere patterned paper around frosting.
2. Stamp dotted label and cupcake on label; affix.

ⓒ SPRINKLES WRAP

1. Stamp dotted label and cupcake on label; affix to sprinkles.
2. Circle-punch patterned paper; adhere to lid.

ⓓ CUPCAKE CUP

1. Die-cut cup from patterned paper; adhere ends together.

ⓔ FAVOR BOX

1. Die-cut favor box and cupcake from cardstock and patterned paper. Assemble and adhere.
2. Stamp dotted tag, for you, and cupcake on cardstock, trim, and adhere.
3. Thread button with twine; adhere. Adhere twine bow.

ⓕ FOOD PICK & HOLDER

1. Die-cut flower from patterned paper; adhere to toothpick.
2. Stamp dotted label and cupcake on label, affix to patterned paper.
3. Trim patterned paper and adhere to box.

ⓖ APRON & HAT

1. Apply interfacing to fabric.
2. Die-cut cupcake and name from fabric.
3. Stamp hearts on white fabric die cut.
4. Iron all die cuts to apron and hat.
5. Die-cut zigzag border from felt; stitch.
6. Stitch button to apron with twine.

ⓗ SERVING BOX

1. Score and fold sides of two 12" x 12" pieces of patterned paper to create top and bottom of box.
2. Use circle cutter to cut circles from top.
3. Stamp flourishes and sentiment on patterned paper. Trim, mat with cardstock, and adhere.
4. Die-cut cupcake from cardstock and patterned paper; adhere together. Thread button with twine and adhere.
5. Adhere panel to box.

Try This

Use this ensemble for a fun and interactive child's birthday party. Make the hats and aprons ahead of time and bake cupcakes as your party activity.

SPRINKLES & smiles

ELIZA

A Tiny Tea Party

Designer: Heidi Van Laar

ⓐ INVITATION

1. Make invitation from cardstock; adhere patterned paper.
2. Round bottom corners and adhere ribbon. Adhere patterned paper rectangle.
3. Trim pink card from patterned paper, print text, and round bottom corners.
4. Affix tab to panel, affix heart, and adhere panel to card.
5. Pleat crepe paper; adhere. Tie ribbon bow and adhere.
6. Affix stickers to spell "Tea party". Thread buttons with twine; adhere.

ⓑ THANK YOU CARD

1. Make card from cardstock; adhere patterned paper.
2. Round bottom corners; adhere ribbon and twine.
3. Affix frame to patterned paper; trim. Affix stickers to spell "Thank you" and adhere panel to card.
4. Affix heart. Thread button with twine; adhere.

ⓒ FOOD PICK

1. Trim designs from patterned paper. Adhere around toothpick.
2. Trim and layer crepe paper; attach brad. Adhere to toothpick.

ⓓ SPOON TOPPER

1. Pleat crepe paper; adhere to spoon.
2. Affix scalloped circle.
3. Thread button with twine; adhere.

ⓔ GARLAND

1. Trim patterned paper strips. Border-punch several strips.
2. Adhere together to create chain.
3. Tie ribbon bows. Tie on buttons with twine and adhere.

ⓕ HEAD BAND

1. Trim and adhere patterned paper to head band. Seal with decoupage.
2. Trim and adhere felt to underside of head band.
3. Pleat and layer crepe paper; adhere.
4. Affix circle and scalloped circle.
5. Tie ribbon bow. Tie on button with twine and adhere.

ⓖ PURSE FAVOR BOX

1. Remove knob from purse, paint, and let dry.
2. Cover purse with patterned paper; sand edges.
3. Hole-punch top flap and tie on ribbon. Tie on tag with twine.
4. Trim spiraled circle from patterned paper, roll, and adhere to create flower. Trim leaves from patterned paper. Adhere leaves and flower.
5. Trim patterned paper circle, adhere to knob, and adhere to purse.

ⓗ CUPCAKE CUP

1. Cut cup from patterned paper using the pattern on included CD.
2. Pleat crepe paper and adhere.

ⓘ CUPCAKE STAND

1. Paint wood disk and candle holder; let dry.
2. Adhere patterned paper to disk.
3. Border-punch patterned paper strip, adhere to edge of disk, and adhere trim.
4. Tie ribbon bow. Tie on button with twine and adhere.
5. Adhere candleholder.

Designer Tip

When covering a curved surface with paper, make sure you cut small notches along the edges so it will more easily follow the contours of your item.

Try This

Make these darling headbands at the party or create them ahead of time and include them with the invites. Ask each guest to wear their tea time finest—a frilly dress and their headband!

thank you

please come to my

tea party

Children's Game Night

Designer: Anabelle O'Malley

ⓐ INVITATION

1. Make card from cardstock.
2. Mat bingo card with specialty paper; trim with decorative-edge scissors.
3. Mat panel with patterned paper and adhere to card.
4. Print text on cardstock, trim, and adhere with foam tape.
5. Adhere game spinner with foam tape.

ⓑ FAVOR BAG

1. Trim patterned paper strip with decorative-edge scissors; adhere to bag.
2. Adhere patterned paper rectangle.
3. Fold bag top, thread button with twine, and adhere.

ⓒ BINGO BOX

1. Adhere patterned paper to box top, lid, and base.
2. Adhere bingo card.

See detailed image of Bingo Box on p. 283

ⓓ HAT

1. Trim specialty paper and adhere cone shape using pattern found on included CD.
2. Trim crepe paper into strips; adhere.
3. Adhere die cuts.

ⓔ BANNER

1. Paint pennants; let dry.
2. Trim triangles from patterned paper; adhere.
3. Adhere chipboard letters to spell "Play" with foam tape.
4. Border-punch specialty paper and patterned paper strips; accordion-fold.
5. Adhere specialty paper strips to pennants. Adhere patterned paper strips together to create flowers.
6. Adhere die cuts to flowers; adhere to pennants.
7. Thread pennants on string.

ⓕ RIBBON

1. Trim patterned paper strip with decorative-edge scissors; accordion-fold.
2. Adhere strip together to create flower.
3. Circle-punch cardstock and scalloped-circle punch patterned paper; adhere together.
4. Trim ribbons from patterned paper; adhere behind panel. Adhere to flower.
5. Print text on cardstock, trim, and adhere with foam tape.
6. Trim and adhere ribbon and patterned paper strips. Adhere behind flower.
7. Repeat for remaining ribbons.

Try This

Invite your favorite little ones over for a night of Candy Land, Chutes and Ladders, Checkers, and more!

White Elephant Gift Exchange

Designer: Laura O'Donnell

(a) INVITATION

1. Make card from cardstock.
2. Print text on cardstock, trim slightly smaller than card front and adhere.
3. Print presents and elephant on specialty paper, trim, apply glitter, and adhere with foam tape.

(b) MENU

1. Print text on cardstock. Trim and mat with cardstock.
2. Draw line with marker; apply glitter.
3. Print present and elephant on specialty paper. Trim and adhere with foam tape. *Note: Apply glitter to present before adhering.*
4. Adhere patterned paper strip and affix sticker.

(c) CUPCAKE TOPPER

1. Circle-punch cardstock.
2. Print elephant and presents on specialty paper. Trim, apply glitter, and adhere to circle with foam tape.
3. Adhere toothpick to circle.
4. Repeat for remaining toppers.

(d) WINE GLASS CHARM

1. Print elephant and presents on specialty paper. Trim, apply glitter, and adhere to tags.
2. Repeat for remaining toppers.

(e) TAG

1. Print "Pick one" on cardstock. Circle-punch.
2. Print elephant on specialty paper, trim, and adhere with foam tape.
3. Hole-punch and attach to can with ball chain.

(f) DRAWING CARD

1. Make card from cardstock; notch-punch.
2. Print present on specialty paper, trim, apply glitter, and adhere.

Designer Tip

Font used in these projects found on included CD.

Try This

Invite your guests to bring a silly, inexpensive (wrapped) gift. Number each present upon arrival. Then have each person pick a number from the can to determine which gift they will unwrap. Once all the gifts have been unwrapped set a time limit and begin exchanging gifts. The gifts don't cost much, and the inevitable laughter they'll invoke will be free of charge!

menu

cosmos

cookies

cupcakes

pick one

it's a white elephant gift exchange

Let's Watch the Oscars

Designer: Becky Olsen

ⓐ INVITATION

1. Mat patterned paper with patterned paper.
2. Print text on patterned paper, mat with patterned paper, and adhere.
3. Trim patterned paper; adhere.
4. Trim tickets from patterned paper; adhere.
5. Adhere rhinestone star.

ⓑ MENU

1. Mat patterned paper square with patterned paper.
2. Print text on patterned paper, trim, and adhere with foam tape.
3. Trim patterned paper strips, curl, and adhere with foam tape.
4. Adhere rhinestone star.

ⓒ FOOD PICK

1. Die-cut label from patterned paper.
2. Print text on patterned paper, die-cut into label, and adhere.
3. Adhere rhinestones to panel and adhere panel to toothpick.

ⓓ NAPKIN RING

1. Die-cut label from patterned paper.
2. Print name on patterned paper, die-cut into circle, and adhere with foam tape.
3. Trim ticket from patterned paper; adhere.
4. Curl label and adhere ends to patterned paper strip to create ring.

ⓔ FAVOR BOX

1. Make box from patterned paper, following pattern found on CD. Assemble.
2. Cut two pieces of 1" x 12" patterned paper. Score every 1⅛", adhere to tabs, and adhere end to end.
3. Slide box top and bottom together.
4. Trim patterned paper and tie to box with ribbon.

ⓕ CENTERPIECE

1. Cut stars from patterned paper. *Note: Fold two stars.*
2. Accordion-fold patterned paper strip. Adhere together to create flower. Adhere stars and flower together.
3. Adhere patterned paper together to create tube. Cut small slits in bottom to create base. Adhere base to stars and flower.
4. Trim patterned paper strips, adhere together, and curl. Adhere top to paper tube.
5. Adhere folded stars to skewer. Insert skewer into tube.

ⓖ BANNER

1. Cut stars from patterned paper.
2. Accordion-fold patterned paper strips. Adhere together to create flowers. Adhere stars and flower together.
3. Adhere rhinestone letters to spell "Star".
4. Tie panels together with ribbon.

Try This

Have a celebrity lookalike contest. Create mini centerpieces to give as awards.

(g)

(f)

(b)

Best Lead-in
Brad Olive Pitt Plate

Best Main Dish
Tom Lamb a Hanks

Best Supporting Dish
Brittney Broccoli Spears

Best Scenery
Leonardo Di Caprese

Best Sweet Treat
Halle Berries and Cream

CLARA BOW

(a)

ON WITH
the SHOW

CINEMA

Please join us for
an evening of
star gazing,
and celebrating
the achievements
of movie making
icons. The red
carpet unrolls
at 6:30 p.m.

Halle Berries and Cream

(c)

Leonardo Di Caprese

(d)

(e)

Murder Mystery Who Dunnit?

Designer: Kim Kesti

ⓐ INVITATION

1. Make invitation from cardstock.
2. Trim patterned paper slightly smaller than card front; adhere.
3. Adhere flower to card and color ribbon with ink and marker.
4. Trim tag from patterned paper. Tie on ribbon and key; adhere with foam tape.
5. Print text on cardstock, trim into label, ink, and mat with patterned paper. Trim, attach brads, and adhere with foam tape.
6. Print text on cardstock, ink, and mat with patterned paper. Adhere.
7. Trim butterfly from patterned paper; adhere.
8. Spritz card with shimmer spray.

ⓑ CAST LIST

1. Print text on cardstock, trim, and double-mat with patterned paper and cardstock.
2. Adhere patterned paper strip and attach brads.
3. Color ribbon with ink and marker, tie to spoon, and adhere.
4. Spritz panel with shimmer spray.

ⓒ CLUE TAGS

1. Stamp number on tag.
2. Trim image from patterned paper; adhere.
3. Spritz tag with shimmer spray.
4. Repeat for remaining tags.
5. Trim image from patterned paper; adhere to clock. Tie tags and clock together with string.

ⓓ NOTEBOOK FAVOR

1. Trim chipboard and cardstock to finished size.
2. Adhere patterned paper to chipboard; ink edges.
3. Trim images from patterned paper, ink edges, and adhere.
4. Bind panels together with binding coil.
5. Color ribbon with ink and marker; tie onto binding.
6. Thread button with twine; adhere.
7. Attach gold clip.

ⓔ SIGN IN BOOK

1. Trim two panels from chipboard; adhere patterned paper rectangles. Ink edges.
2. Bind panels together with binding coils.
3. Print "Guest sign in" on cardstock; insert into bookplate.
4. Attach medallion to bookplate and adhere to book.
5. Color ribbon with ink and marker; tie to medallion.
6. Spritz book with shimmer spray.

Try This

Write your own murder mystery plot or purchase a predesigned kit at your local game store. Assign guests characters and costumes prior to the party and serve one course of the meal between each clue reading in order to keep your party interactive and tasty!

a

Murder of a
Steampunk Debutante

Mystery Dinner Party

b

Cast of Characters

Edwinna W. Murdock
Lord Joshua J. Rivington
Professor Newlock
Ms. Smythe-White
Bridget Dargon
Inspector Renton Cogley

c

d

Worthington
STEAM PUNKS

MODELLER
AERO

10 MURRAY STREET
NEW YORK.

See The Valley From The Air
Guaranteed Solo Course, 15

THE ORIGINAL.
AL·METAL·POLISHIN
KRUMA

e

Guest Sign In

Wine Tasting Party

Designer: Michelle Keeth, courtesy of Canvas Corp

ⓐ INVITATION

1. Make gate-fold invitation from patterned paper; ink.
2. Trim specialty paper strip with decorative-edge scissors. Ink edges and adhere.
3. Stamp Text on patterned paper, tear edges, and ink. Adhere.
4. Attach loop brads and tie on twine.
5. Print invitation wording on Kraft and mat with patterned paper; adhere following pattern found on included CD.

ⓑ FOOD FLAG

1. Trim flags from patterned paper; ink.
2. Adhere flags to toothpicks.
3. Trim specialty paper with decorative-edge scissors; adhere.

ⓒ DRINK CHARM

1. Stamp monogram on cork; circle-punch.
2. Stamp Text on patterned paper, trim with decorative-edge scissors, and adhere to cork circle.
3. Hole-punch and tie on twine.

ⓓ BOTTLE WRAP

1. Trim patterned paper to finished size; ink edges.
2. Trim patterned paper strip. Tear and ink edges; adhere.
3. Circle-punch cork, stamp monogram, and adhere.
4. Adhere around bottle.

ⓔ TALLY BOARD

1. Trim matte board to finished size; ink.
2. Print text on cardstock, trim, ink edges, and mat with patterned paper. Ink edges.
3. Ink edges of patterned paper rectangle; adhere to board.
4. Attach clothespins to printed panel; adhere.
5. Cut wine cork in half; adhere.

ⓕ GUIDE BOOK

1. Fold gift bags in half. Trim off all but one handle.
2. Stamp Text on patterned paper, tear edge, and ink. Adhere.
3. Trim patterned paper rectangle, ink edges, and adhere.
4. Trim patterned paper into wine bottle shape. Trim cork; adhere. Ink edges of panel and adhere.
5. Trim patterned paper; adhere.
6. Stamp Wine Glass on cork, trim, and adhere.
7. Layer folded bags, ink all edges, and hole-punch. Attach binder rings.
8. Adhere cord around handle. Embellish remaining pages as desired.

See inside image of guide book on p. 283.

ⓖ CENTERPIECE

Large Panel
Ink all edges.

1. Adhere cardstock rectangle to frame.
2. Crumple and smooth patterned paper; adhere.
3. Stamp text on patterned paper strip, tear edges, and adhere.
4. Using pattern included on CD, trim wine bottle, glass, and wine shapes from patterned paper; adhere.
5. Print wine label on cardstock, trim, and adhere.
6. Cut wine cork in half; adhere.

Small Panels
Ink all edges.

1. Trim patterned paper strips; adhere inside frames.
2. Stamp Text on patterned paper, trim into strips, and adhere to frames.
3. Stamp typewriter text and Clock on cork square; adhere inside frame.
4. Bend fork, tie on twine, adhere wine cork, and adhere to frame.
5. Adhere patterned paper square to mini canvas; adhere.
6. Adhere wine corks inside frame. Adhere knife.

Assemble

1. Attach hinges with tacks and attach hinges together with pins.
2. Tie on charm with twine.

Designer Tip

The invitation wording and wine bottle label can be found on included CD.

Try This

Serve an assortment of cheeses and fruit alongside your wine. Label your items by writing their names on your chalkboard food flags.

ⓒ
DRINK
CHARM

Backyard Carnival Bonanza

Designer: Julie Campbell

ⓐ INVITATION

1. Make invitation from cardstock.
2. Mat patterned paper rectangle with cardstock; adhere.
3. Print text on cardstock. Stamp handlebar moustache and color text with markers.
4. Trim and circle-punch panel, mat with cardstock, circle-punch, and adhere.

ⓑ MOUSTACHE PICK

1. Stamp handlebar moustaches on cardstock, trim, and adhere together with foam tape.
2. Adhere to dowel.

ⓒ CUPCAKE CUP

1. Die-cut cupcake liner from patterned paper; adhere ends together.

ⓓ BANNER

1. Paint pennants; let dry.
2. Stamp letters to spell "Party"; emboss.
3. Thread pennants on twine.

ⓔ CENTERPIECE

1. Remove top tier from cupcake stand.
2. Adhere cardstock to pedestals and apply glitter to edges.
3. Adhere patterned paper to base; adhere tickets around edge.
4. Cut small slits in stand and insert carousel horse; adhere.
5. Trim and stitch patterned paper triangles. Adhere into cone shape.
6. Die-cut cupcake liners from patterned paper. Adhere to inside of cone to create border. Adhere trim.
7. Trim patterned paper, adhere around stick pin, and insert in cone.
8. Assemble stand, pedestal, and cone.

Designer Tips

- Use circle punches to create half circles in your cardstock. With a few quick punches you'll have custom tags and labels that look just like die cuts.

- Invite wording can be found on included CD.

Try This

Gather your friends for an afternoon of classic carnival games including balloon pop and ring toss. Serve cotton candy, popcorn, corn dogs, and lemonade.

Cinco De Mayo

Designer: Kim Kesti

ⓐ INVITATION

1. Make invitation from cardstock; adhere patterned paper rectangle.
2. Adhere cardstock to chipboard banner. Adhere crepe paper behind piece, and mat with cardstock. Adhere.
3. Adhere patterned paper strip to cardstock rectangle. Affix border sticker and letters to spell "Fiesta". Adhere to card with foam tape.
4. Adhere bird with foam tape.

ⓑ THANK YOU CARD

1. Make card from cardstock.
2. Border-punch patterned paper rectangle; adhere.
3. Print "Moustache gracias" on cardstock, trim, and adhere.
4. Adhere patterned paper to chipboard banner; adhere.
5. Affix piñata with foam tape.
6. Trim moustache from cardstock; adhere.

ⓒ FOOD PICK

1. Print text on cardstock; trim.
2. Border-punch patterned paper rectangle; adhere.
3. Adhere pepper with foam tape and adhere panel to skewer.
4. Repeat for remaining picks.

ⓓ BAG TOPPER

1. Make bag topper from patterned paper.
2. Adhere cardstock strip and affix letters to spell "Dulces".
3. Trim half circles from cardstock, adhere together, and adhere to topper. Adhere dog with foam tape.

ⓔ BANNER

1. Trim rectangles from specialty and patterned paper.
2. Border-punch patterned paper.
3. Spritz specialty paper with shimmer spray; let dry.
4. Stitch panels to twill.
5. Pleat crepe paper; adhere. Adhere button. Trim border sticker; affix.

Try This

Create a make-shift photo booth at your party. Provide sombreros, ponchos, and paper moustaches as props and let your guests' creativity do the rest!

e

b

MUSTACHE
GRACIAS

d

DULCES

a

FiESTa

TAMALE
(Tuh-mah-lee)

CHIMICHANGA
(Chim-ee-chahng-guh)

c

QUESADILLA
(Kay-suh-dee-uh)

Frankly, My Dear... Soiree

Designer: Sarah Jay

ⓐ INVITATION

❶ Print text on patterned paper, trim, and color text with marker.
❷ Print frame on cardstock, trim, and adhere.
❸ Stamp moustache on cardstock, adhere flock, trim, and adhere with foam tape.

ⓑ NOTEBOOK FAVOR

❶ Adhere patterned paper to notebook.
❷ Affix label and border.
❸ Stamp sentiment on label.
❹ Stamp moustache on cardstock, adhere flock, and trim. Adhere.

ⓒ FOOD LABEL

❶ Print "Peach cobbler" on patterned paper; trim.
❷ Print frame on cardstock, trim, and adhere.
❸ Stamp moustache on cardstock, adhere flock, and trim. Adhere with foam tape.
❹ Adhere panel to frame.

ⓓ CUPCAKE TOPPER

❶ Circle-punch patterned paper; stamp sentiment.
❷ Stamp moustache on cardstock, adhere flock, and trim. Adhere with foam tape.
❸ Adhere panel to toothpick.

ⓔ CUPCAKE CUP

❶ Using pattern included on CD; cut cup from patterned paper; adhere.

ⓕ DRINK LABEL

❶ Stamp moustache on label; affix to cup.

Designer Tip

The invitation template can be found on the included CD.

Try This

- The movie *Gone with the Wind* is nearly four hours long, so plan enough time for guests to eat, drink, and enjoy an intermission.

- Prepare some movie trivia to entertain your guests before the flick begins.

a

You're invited to
a private screening of
the most magnificent picture of all time
GONE WITH THE WIND
Saturday, January 21 at 7pm
The Wilkersons House · 16 Tara Drive

RSVP to Melanie   Brief Intermission
555-987-6543   Drinks & Snacks

Sean

aila

f   amy

d   FRANKLY,
    MY DEAR...

b   FRANKLY,
    MY DEAR...

FRANKLY,
MY DEAR...

e

PEACH
COBBLER

c

Festive Mardi Gras

Designer: Teri Anderson

(a) INVITATION

1. Print text on cardstock, trim, and double-mat with cardstock.
2. Hole-punch and tie on beads with ribbon. Adhere rhinestones.

(b) FOOD LABEL

1. Make food label from cardstock; adhere cardstock strips.
2. Print text on cardstock, trim, and adhere.
3. Stamp crown on cardstock, trim, and adhere.
4. Adhere rhinestones.

(c) NAPKIN RING

1. Adhere cardstock strips together.
2. Adhere rhinestones and adhere ends to create ring.

(d) BAG TOPPER

1. Make topper from cardstock; adhere cardstock strips.
2. Print sentiment on cardstock, trim, and adhere.
3. Stamp crown on cardstock, trim, and adhere. Adhere rhinestones.

(e) DRINK CHARM

1. Circle-punch cardstock. Adhere cardstock strips.
2. Affix sticker and adhere rhinestones.
3. Hole-punch, attach binder ring, and tie on ribbon.

(f) HORN

1. Adhere cardstock strip and rhinestones to horn.
2. Tie on ribbon.

(g) CROWN

1. Adhere cardstock strips together. Adhere ends to create circle.
2. Trim triangles from cardstock using pattern found on CD; adhere.
3. Adhere rhinestones.

Designer Tip

Save time and money by dressing up store bought horns with rhinestones and ribbon.

Try This

Begin your party with music and dancing and end the night by crowning a Mardi Gras king and queen.

Hot Crab Dip

ⓑ

Jambalaya

Muffalettas

Bread Pudding

ⓐ

Bring on the beads!
It is Mardi Gras time
and we are celebrating in a big way!

We would love for you to join us.

We will dine on Gumbo and King Cake!
We will crown a queen and king!
And we will hand out beads and coins.

The festivities start at 5 p.m.

The LaRoche house
555-1212
Regrets only.

ⓔ

ⓓ

Thanks for celebrating with us!

ⓕ

ⓒ

ⓖ

Shaken, Not Stirred

Designer: Susan R. Opel

ⓐ INVITATION

1. Print text on cardstock; trim. Adhere cardstock and patterned paper rectangles to panel.
2. Double-mat panel with cardstock.
3. Circle-punch hat from patterned paper, adhere rhinestones, and adhere to invitation with foam tape.

ⓑ DRINK CHARM

1. Hole-punch doily die cut; attach earring.

ⓒ FRAME

1. Paint edges of frame; let dry.
2. Adhere patterned paper and cardstock strips.
3. Adhere rhinestones and insert photo.

ⓓ CD FAVOR

1. Trim cardstock to fit inside CD case; adhere cardstock and patterned paper strips.
2. Adhere cardstock and patterned paper strips together, trim, corner-punch, and affix stickers to spell "Crooner tunes". Adhere.
3. Adhere rhinestones and insert panel inside CD case.

ⓔ GARNISH

1. Cut ovals from cardstock, adhere rhinestones, and adhere together.
2. Adhere panel to dowel.

ⓕ BANNER

1. Adhere cardstock to pennants.
2. Adhere cardstock and patterned paper strips.
3. Print "Cheers!" on cardstock, circle-punch, and adhere to pennants with foam tape.
4. Adhere rhinestones, hole-punch pennants, and thread pennants on ribbon.

Designer Tip

The "cheers" letters can be found on included CD.

Try This

- Place your paper garnish in an oversized martini glass for a fun centerpiece.

- Send each guest home with a CD filled with retro music. Play the CD at the party to make the music even more memorable!

DRINK CHARM

You're invited to a

Retro Cocktail Party

We promise you'll be
shaken not stirred by all of the fun!

Where: Our House
When: Friday from 8 pm - ?
What to bring: A martini shaker

RSVP: Give us a ring-a-ding-ding!

Craft Night

Designer: Jennifer McGuire

ⓐ INVITATION

❶ Make invitation from cardstock; stamp buttons.

❷ Adhere patterned paper and cardstock strips. Stitch border and round corners.

❸ Print sentiment on cardstock, stamp rectangle border, and trim.

❹ Ink panel edges, stitch on buttons, and adhere to invitation with foam tape.

ⓑ CUP COZY

❶ Trim cardstock to finished size. *Note: Angle cardstock to fit around cup.*

❷ Stamp buttons on panel and mat with cardstock.

❸ Print name on cardstock, trim, round corners, and ink edges. Adhere.

❹ Stitch on buttons and adhere ends together.

ⓒ FAVOR CARDS

❶ Stamp borders, sentiments, and labels on cardstock. Ink edges and round corners.

❷ Die-cut notch from some cards.

❸ Stitch on buttons, attach trim with safety pins, and adhere flowers.

ⓓ CANDY TAG

❶ Print sentiment and name on cardstock.

❷ Stamp rectangle border, homespun quality, and zigzag border on panel.

❸ Trim panel, round corners, and ink edges.

❹ Adhere flowers and stitch with thread.

❺ Hole-punch and tie on ribbon.

ⓔ PLACE CARD

❶ Make place setting from cardstock.

❷ Print sentiment and name on cardstock.

❸ Stamp rectangle border and label on panel. Trim, ink edges, and adhere to place setting.

❹ Thread buttons and adhere.

ⓕ GIFT BAG

❶ Stamp buttons on gift bag and border-punch top.

❷ Adhere patterned paper and cardstock strips.

❸ Print sentiment and name on cardstock; die-cut notch.

❹ Stamp rectangle border, craft worthy, and dotted line on panel.

❺ Trim, ink edges, and adhere stitched buttons.

❻ Adhere panel to bag with foam tape.

Try This

Have everyone bring craft supplies to swap. At the end of the night, guests will have "new" product to play with.

Joy in the Garden

Designer: Betsy Veldman

ⓐ INVITATION ENVELOPE

1. Make envelope from patterned paper, following pattern found on CD. Ink edges.
2. Trim images from patterned paper; adhere.
3. Stamp you're invited on flap.
4. Circle-punch cardstock, ink edges, and attach with brads.
5. Tie on twine and button.

ⓑ INVITATION INSERT

1. Trim image from patterned paper, mat with cardstock, and ink edges. Hole-punch.
2. Print text on vellum, trim with decorative-edge scissors, and hole-punch.
3. Tie panels together with ribbon.

ⓒ NOTEBOOK

1. Adhere patterned paper to notebook cover. Ink edges.
2. Ink envelope and adhere.
3. Trim image from patterned paper; ink edges and adhere.
4. Stamp rectangle label and journal on cardstock, ink, trim, and adhere.
5. Tie on twine.

ⓓ CLAY POT FAVOR

1. Stamp sentiment on envelope, ink edges, and adhere patterned paper.
2. Tie on twine and button.
3. Adhere dowel.
4. Paint clay pot and insert embellished dowel.

ⓔ CENTERPIECE

1. Paint clay pot; plant flowers.

ⓕ NAPKIN RING

1. Trim image from patterned paper; hole-punch.
2. Tie patterned paper to wreath with ribbon.

ⓖ PLACE SETTING

1. Adhere patterned paper strip to pot; tie on ribbon.
2. Trim image from patterned paper, distress edges, and adhere to dowel.
3. Trim spring from wreath and adhere.
4. Print name on cardstock, trim, and ink edges. Adhere.
5. Insert into pot.

Try This

- Plant greenery or flowers in clay pots. Write the name of the plant with chalk along the painted rims.

- Fill place setting pots with candy for a yummy after dinner treat.

PANSY

RASPBERRY

Cultivated just for you

Bloom where you are planted

ORANGE BUI
WEBSTER SEED HOUSE

ORANGE BUI
WEBSTER SEED HOUSE

ⓔ

SWEET PEA

PANSY

Yvonne

Violet

ⓖ

Pansies

ⓓ

Roses

Harvest

SEED ANNUAL

Journal

ⓒ

RAMBOISE

ⓕ

You're invited

Garden Party

Where: My Backyard

When: July 26 at 3:00 pm

Bring some cuttings to share

ⓐ

RASPBERRY

GATHERING
WEBSTER SEED HOUSE CO.

ⓑ

Love to Read Book Club

Designer: Anabelle O'Malley

ⓐ INVITATION

1. Make invitation from patterned paper.
2. Print text on cardstock, trim, ink edges, and adhere.
3. Border-punch patterned paper strip; adhere.
4. Stamp book on patterned paper, trim, and adhere with foam tape.

ⓑ FAVOR BAG

1. Adhere patterned paper rectangles to bag; ink edges.
2. Border-punch patterned paper strips; adhere. Tie on twill.
3. Affix stickers to sticker label to spell "Cookies". Adhere to bag with foam tape.

ⓒ NOTEBOOK

1. Adhere patterned paper to notebook cover. Ink edges.
2. Stamp sentiment on patterned paper rectangle; adhere.
3. Border-punch patterned paper strip; adhere.
4. Affix label sticker and alphabet stickers to spell "Notes". Attach brad.

ⓓ BOOK PLATE

1. Mat patterned paper rectangle with cardstock; ink edges.
2. Adhere patterned paper rectangle.
3. Die-cut label from cardstock. Stamp round grid label, silhouetted circle, and sentiment.
4. Ink edges of panel and adhere.
5. Border-punch patterned paper strip; adhere.

ⓔ CUP COZY

1. Trim patterned paper to finished size; ink edges.
2. Die-cut label from cardstock. Stamp round grid label and silhouetted circle. Ink edges.
3. Affix label sticker and write name with marker.
4. Adhere stamped piece.

ⓕ BOOKMARK

1. Mat patterned paper with cardstock; ink edges.
2. Border-punch cardstock strip; adhere.
3. Stamp sentiment. Affix label and alphabet stickers.
4. Stamp silhouetted circle on cardstock; circle-punch.
5. Punch scalloped circle from patterned paper, adhere stamped circle, and adhere to bookmark with foam tape.
6. Attach twill with brad.

Try This

Encourage your club members to jot down thoughts in their notebook and then bring it to future parties to share their insights.

(a)

Time for Book Club!

Hope you can join us this month.
April 4 at 7 pm
At Anabelle's

Can't wait to hear your thoughts
about the book.

(b) cookies

(e) Anabelle ♡

(f) This is where I fell ASLEEP

ENJOY

READ

(c) NOTES

A book is like a garden carried in the pocket. ~CHINESE PROVERB

(d)

Jane Austen Book Club

Designer: Angie Tieman

ⓐ WALL HANGING

1. Paint wreath frame; let dry.
2. Adhere tulle and ribbon behind wreath.
3. Print silhouette on patterned paper, trim into circle, and ink edges. Adhere to patterned paper.
4. Affix flag stickers to chipboard flags; adhere to panel.
5. Stamp stitched pennant on book page, trim, and adhere to chipboard banner. Adhere to flags.
6. Attach floss to panel with brads. Adhere pearls.
7. Adhere pennants to panel with foam tape. Affix alphabet to spell "Austen."
8. Adhere panel to wreath.

ⓑ NOTEBOOK

1. Trim patterned paper to finished size to create cover.
2. Border-punch strip from book page; adhere.
3. Adhere alphabet to spell "Notes & quotes".
4. Paint silhouette, oval, and frame; let dry.
5. Adhere book page to oval. Adhere frame, oval, and silhouette to panel.
6. Tie cover and patterned paper together with ribbon.

ⓒ PENCIL

1. Adhere book page to pencil.
2. Paint silhouettes; let dry.
3. Insert stick pin in eraser and adhere silhouettes.
4. Adhere trim.

ⓓ RIBBON BOOKMARK

1. Pleat and adhere ribbon and trim to patterned paper strip.
2. Paint silhouette and oval; let dry.
3. Adhere patterned paper to oval and adhere silhouette. Adhere pearls.
4. Adhere lace behind oval and adhere to bookmark.
5. Insert stick pin.

ⓔ PLEATED BOOKMARK

1. Pleat book page and stitch to patterned paper rectangle.
2. Die-cut doily from cardstock, trim, and adhere behind image trimmed from patterned paper; adhere.
3. Thread lace on stick pin; adhere.
4. Affix flag sticker to chipboard; adhere.
5. Adhere buttons and pearls.

ⓕ FAVOR BAG

1. Emboss bag and trim top with decorative-edge scissors.
2. Die-cut doily from patterned paper. Circle-punch book page and adhere. Adhere panel to bag.
3. Paint chipboard oval; let dry. Adhere patterned paper and pearls.
4. Trim flower trim; adhere. Adhere chipboard oval.

ⓖ PLACE SETTING

1. Oval-punch patterned paper and cardstock. Adhere to toothpicks.
2. Affix flag sticker to chipboard; adhere to toothpick.
3. Adhere book page to spool.
4. Tie on ribbon and insert stick pin.
5. Insert oval and flag into spool. *Note: Adhere pearls to some ovals.*

ⓗ CROWN

1. Make crown from patterned paper, following template.
2. Paint frame and oval; let dry.
3. Adhere patterned paper to oval. Adhere pearls.
4. Adhere frame and oval to crown.
5. Adhere ribbon, trim, and rhinestones.
6. Adhere ends to create crown.

Try This

Print Jane Austen quotes on cardstock panels and use them as decorations for the inside pages of your notebook.

ⓖ
PLACE SETTING

Sew Much Fun

Designer: Julia Stainton

ⓐ INVITATION

❶ Make invitation from cardstock; ink edges.

❷ Adhere patterned paper squares together, mat with cardstock, and stitch seams and borders.

❸ Trim panel with decorative-edge scissors and adhere to card.

❹ Knot lace and adhere.

❺ Die-cut flowers from sewing pattern. Staple together and adhere. Insert stick pins.

ⓑ NAPKIN RING

❶ Trim patterned paper strip.

❷ Adhere measuring tape and staple to create ring.

❸ Tie on button with twine.

ⓒ PLACE CARD

❶ Adhere patterned paper to spool.

❷ Thread buttons on stick pin and insert into spool.

❸ Write name on cardstock strip with marker. Insert in stick pin.

ⓓ FAVOR FOLDER

❶ Cut rectangle from patterned paper. Fold up bottom flap and fold in half to create folder.

❷ Adhere doily and tie on ribbon.

❸ Adhere flowers and insert stick pin.

ⓔ BANNER

❶ Trim half circles from patterned paper. Mat with cardstock.

❷ Stitch border and trim with decorative-edge scissors.

❸ Trim sewing pattern strips with decorative-edge scissors. Pleat and adhere to panels.

❹ Hole-punch panels and thread on ribbon. Adhere flower.

ⓕ CENTERPIECE BOX & INSERTS

❶ Adhere patterned paper and measuring tape to outside of box.

❷ Fill inside of box with foam and sewing pattern.

❸ Trim square from patterned paper. Cut diagonal lines from corners into center.

❹ Adhere alternating ends to center.

❺ Adhere button and skewer.

❻ Circle-punch cardstock; adhere flower.

❼ Place inserts into foam.

Try This

- Fill your favor folders with carded pins and buttons for a practical and cute take-home for your guests.

- Use an old quilt as the tablecloth for your party.

ⓒ
PLACE SETTING

Coffee Break

Designer: Laura Williams

ⓐ INVITATION

1. Make invitation from cardstock.
2. Mat patterned paper with cardstock; adhere.
3. Mat patterned paper with cardstock, border-punch edges, and adhere.
4. Print text on cardstock, trim, mat with cardstock, and adhere.
5. Stamp cup and saucer on patterned paper and cardstock; trim and adhere.
6. Tie button to ribbon bow with twine. Adhere.

ⓑ THANKS CARD

1. Make invitation from cardstock.
2. Mat patterned paper with cardstock and adhere.
3. Mat cardstock square with patterned paper. Tie on twine and button.
4. Mat panel with cardstock and adhere.
5. Stamp sentiment on cardstock, trim, and mat with cardstock; trim. Adhere to card.
6. Stamp cup and saucer on cardstock, trim, and adhere with foam tape.

ⓒ DRINK LABEL

1. Make drink label from cardstock; adhere patterned paper.
2. Border-punch cardstock strip; adhere.
3. Stamp cup and saucer on cardstock, trim, and adhere.
4. Affix stickers to spell sentiment.
5. Tie on button with twine.

ⓓ MENU CARD

1. Make card from cardstock; adhere patterned paper.
2. Print text on cardstock, trim, and mat with cardstock. Border-punch bottom edge; adhere.
3. Draw small heart with marker.
4. Stamp plated muffins on cardstock and patterned paper. Trim and adhere.
5. Trim flowers from patterned paper and cardstock with decorative-edge scissors; adhere together.
6. Tie on ribbon and adhere circle.
7. Thread button with twine and adhere.

ⓔ CENTERPIECE

1. Mat patterned paper with cardstock; adhere to chipboard rectangle.
2. Adhere patterned paper strip.
3. Affix stickers to cardstock rectangle to spell sentiment; tie on twine. Mat with cardstock and border-punch bottom edge.
4. Trim flowers from patterned paper, tissue paper, and cardstock with decorative-edge scissors; adhere.
5. Thread button with twine and adhere.
6. Adhere chipboard woman. Adhere panel.

ⓕ CUPCAKE CUP

1. Make cup from cardstock, following template.
2. Hole-punch scallops and adhere patterned paper.
3. Adhere together to create cup.

ⓖ NAPKIN RING

1. Trim patterned paper to finished size.
2. Adhere to create ring.
3. Tie on ribbon and twine.
4. Thread button with twine; adhere.

ⓗ FAVOR WRAP

1. Trim patterned paper to finished size.
2. Stamp cool beans circle on cardstock; trim.
3. Circle-punch cardstock, adhere stamped image, and adhere to panel.
4. Adhere and tie ribbon. Thread button with twine and adhere.

Try This

Brew up several types of coffee to please any guest, and provide creamers in a variety of special flavors.

e Get It whiLe it's HoT!

b Thanks a Latte!

d sweet eats
♥
gingerbread biscotti
carrot cupcakes
chocolate-dipped strawberries
shortbread cookies
lemon streusel muffins

c r e g u l a r

c d e c a f

a please come for coffee

f

g

h

All Girl Craft Night

Designer: Melissa Phillips

ⓐ INVITATION

Ink all edges.

❶ Make invitation from cardstock; paint edges.
❷ Adhere patterned paper rectangles.
❸ Stitch border, stamp sentiment, and adhere lace.
❹ Cut slit in seam and tie on ribbon.
❺ Adhere chipboard flower.
❻ Adhere patterned paper strip to wood spool. Adhere spool to tag.
❼ Tie on tag and button with twine.

ⓑ PLACE SETTING

❶ Adhere lace and button to journaling card.
❷ Stamp name on tag, tie on floss, and clip to panel with clothespin.
❸ Adhere panel to pencil and insert into threaded spool.

ⓒ FAVOR POCKET

❶ Fold book page in half. Ink edges and stitch sides.
❷ Adhere patterned paper rectangle and eyelet trim.
❸ Affix flourish sticker; adhere chipboard label and circle.
❹ Tie on ribbon. Tie on button with twine.

ⓓ CENTERPIECE

❶ Insert fabric into embroidery hoop.
❷ Adhere chipboard sewing machine and lace.
❸ Thread buttons with floss; adhere. Adhere bow with rhinestone.
❹ Adhere floss around spool, thread on stick pin, and insert in fabric. Insert second stick pin.
❺ Affix home sticker.
❻ Tie hoop to jar with ribbon; attach brad.

ⓔ WALL HANGING

❶ Adhere patterned paper rectangles together; stitch border.
❷ Affix alphabet stickers to tags to spell "Create", adhere to panel, and adhere lace.
❸ Stitch buttons to button card; adhere with foam tape. Insert stick pins.
❹ Adhere chipboard flower and label. Adhere spool.
❺ Adhere lace and chipboard circle to hanger.
❻ Clip on panel.

Try This

Fill your favor pocket with button cards, fabric swatches, and a mini embroidery hoop.

Girl's Night In

Designer: Heidi Van Laar

ⓐ INVITATION

❶ Make invitation from cardstock.
❷ Adhere patterned paper rectangles.
❸ Adhere ribbon.
❹ Die-cut label from patterned paper, adhere rhinestones, and adhere to card with foam tape.
❺ Print sentiment on cardstock, trim, adhere trimmed ribbon, and adhere to card with foam tape.

ⓑ BOTTLE WRAP

❶ Cut patterned paper to finished size. Adhere slightly smaller patterned paper rectangle.
❷ Die-cut labels from patterned paper.
❸ Adhere large label, ribbon, and small label.
❹ Affix flower stickers.

ⓒ GLASS FLAG

❶ Print name on patterned paper; trim.
❷ Mat strip with patterned paper; adhere.
❸ Adhere rhinestone and adhere around glass. Trim ends.

ⓓ TREAT CONE

❶ Using pattern included on CD adhere patterned paper into cone shape.
❷ Adhere crepe paper and tie with ribbon.
❸ Affix pinwheel sticker.

ⓔ CORSAGE FAVOR

❶ Trim leaves and flowers from patterned paper. Adhere together with foam tape.
❷ Affix butterfly and adhere rhinestones.
❸ Adhere felt and pin back.

ⓕ NAPKIN RING

❶ Trim patterned paper to finished size.
❷ Adhere patterned paper strip and ribbon.
❸ Adhere to create ring.
❹ Trim and adhere ribbon; affix flower sticker.

ⓖ STIR STICK TOPPER

❶ Trim patterned paper; adhere to stir stick.
❷ Affix pinwheel sticker.

ⓗ ROSETTE WALL DÉCOR

❶ Accordion-fold patterned paper rectangle. Adhere ends to create rosette.
❷ Die-cut scalloped circles from patterned paper; adhere. *Note: Adhere rhinestones to some rosettes.*
❸ Adhere string.

Try This

Dress up your wine bottle even more by adhering a coordinating patterned paper strip around the neck.

Girl's Night In!

Heidi

Savory Recipe Swap

Designer: Kim Kesti

ⓐ INVITATION

❶ Make invitation from cardstock.
❷ Print text on cardstock; adhere.
❸ Adhere patterned paper strips and stitch on rickrack.
❹ Adhere twine bow and attach brad.

ⓑ RECIPE CARD

❶ Print template on cardstock.
❷ Adhere patterned paper strip and stitch rickrack.

ⓒ MENU BOARD

❶ Paint tray; let dry.
❷ Trim patterned paper to fit inside tray; adhere patterned paper strip.
❸ Print text on cardstock; adhere to panel.
❹ Affix borders to panel and stitch on rickrack.
❺ Adhere flower and adhere panel inside tray.

ⓓ RECIPE BOX

❶ Adhere patterned paper to front of recipe box.
❷ Adhere patterned paper to front flap.
❸ Affix border and adhere rickrack.
❹ Adhere flower.

ⓔ FAVOR TAG

❶ Adhere patterned paper rectangles to cardstock square.
❷ Print text on cardstock, trim, and adhere.
❸ Stitch on rickrack.
❹ Adhere twine bow and attach brad.

Try This

Tie your favor tag to an inexpensive stack of measuring cups for a simple take-home gift.

ⓒ

menu
avocado corn salsa & chips
garden chicken chowder with dill
zesty cheese straws
strawberry spinach salad
chocolate lava cake

ⓓ

ⓑ

recipe for:
from the kitchen of:

ⓐ

please join us for a
recipe swap party
february 18, 2012
1pm at amy's place
bring 12 copies of your
favorite recipe
(cards enclosed)
rsvp: amy@gmail.com

ⓔ

a good
friend always
measures up

Girls Only

Designer: Lucy Abrams

ⓐ INVITATION

❶ Make card from cardstock.

❷ Print "Girls' night in" repeatedly on cardstock. Trim and adhere to card; stitch edges.

❸ Stamp leaves and flower on patterned paper. Trim and adhere with foam tape.

❹ Stamp you're invited on card and adhere rhinestone.

ⓑ CUPCAKE BOX

❶ Print "Girls' night in" repeatedly on cardstock.

❷ Trim cardstock, stitch edges, and adhere. Repeat for remaining sides.

❸ Stamp flowers and leaves on patterned paper, trim, and adhere with foam tape.

❹ Adhere rhinestones.

ⓒ GIFT BAG

❶ Print "for" on patterned paper. Trim, stitch edges, and tie on ribbon.

❷ Adhere panel to gift bag.

❸ Stamp you.

❹ Stamp flowers and leaves on patterned paper. Trim and adhere with foam tape.

❺ Adhere rhinestones.

ⓓ CUPCAKE TOPPER

❶ Stamp flowers and leaves on patterned paper. Trim and adhere together with foam tape.

❷ Adhere rhinestone and toothpick.

❸ Print "Girls' night in" repeatedly on cardstock. Print cupcake flavor on cardstock.

❹ Die-cut label from printed cardstock and adhere to toothpick.

ⓔ DRINK LABEL

❶ Make label card from cardstock.

❷ Print "Girls' night in" repeatedly on cardstock. Print drink name on cardstock.

❸ Trim printed cardstock, mat with patterned paper, and stitch border. Adhere.

❹ Stamp flower on patterned paper, trim, and adhere with foam tape.

❺ Adhere rhinestone.

ⓕ FAVOR LABEL

❶ Print "Girls' night in" repeatedly on cardstock.

❷ Die-cut patterned paper and printed cardstock into labels. Adhere together and stitch labels.

❸ Stamp enjoy! on label.

❹ Stamp flower on patterned paper, trim, and adhere with foam tape. Adhere rhinestone.

Designer Tip

The "girls night in" background text can be found on included CD.

Try This

Give your guests a cupcake box, filled with a tasty treat, as a yummy favor.

for
you

enjoy!

COCKTAIL
Blue Hawaii

COCKTAIL
Strawberry Daiquiri

COCKTAIL
Piña Colada

Lemon

Chocolate

Vanilla

you're invited

Picture Perfect

Designer: Windy Robinson

ⓐ INVITATION

1. Make card from cardstock.
2. Adhere patterned paper rectangles and corner-punch bottom.
3. Border-punch cardstock strip; adhere.
4. Adhere rhinestones and affix alphabet stickers to spell "Party".
5. Tie on ribbon.
6. Print "Girls night" on cardstock, trim into tag, and tie onto ribbon with twine. Adhere rhinestone.

ⓑ FRAME

1. Paint frame; let dry.
2. Adhere patterned paper. Stamp medallion border and flourishes.
3. Stamp sentiment on cardstock square. Insert inside frame.
4. Adhere rhinestones.

ⓒ FOOD PICK

1. Adhere flag around beaded stick pin.
2. Thread bead on stick pin and tie on ribbon.

ⓓ GLASS CHARM

1. Stamp starburst on patterned paper, circle-punch, and ink edges.
2. Circle-punch cardstock and adhere stamped piece.
3. Thread crystal charm on jump ring; attach to panel.
4. Thread beads on eye pin; loop around jump ring.
5. Affix sticker and adhere ribbon bow.

ⓔ BOTTLE WRAP

1. Trim patterned paper to finished size. Adhere patterned paper rectangle.
2. Border-punch cardstock strip; adhere.
3. Adhere rhinestones and affix tape.
4. Adhere around bottle.
5. Tie on ribbon.
6. Print "Girls night" on cardstock, trim into tag, and tie onto ribbon with twine. Adhere rhinestone.

ⓕ CAMERA FAVOR WRAP

1. Mat patterned paper strip with cardstock. Border-punch edges.
2. Adhere rhinestones.
3. Adhere around camera.
4. Tie on ribbon.

ⓖ CANDY CONE

1. Adhere patterned paper to create cone.
2. Pleat and adhere ribbon.
3. Adhere rhinestones and tie on ribbon.
4. Print "Girls night" on cardstock, trim into tag, and adhere. Adhere rhinestone.

ⓗ FAN

1. Stamp medallion border on patterned paper rectangle.
2. Accordion-fold panel. Hole-punch bottom and tie together with twine.
3. Thread charms on twine; tie to fan.
4. Stamp always and fabulous on cardstock, trim, and adhere rhinestones. Adhere to fan.

ⓘ CENTERPIECE

1. Paint frame box; let dry.
2. Adhere patterned paper and affix tape.
3. Border-punch cardstock strips; adhere.
4. Insert photos into frame and tie on ribbon.

Try This

Follow up your party with simple thank you notes that include photos taken with your disposable cameras.

ⓓ
GLASS CHARM

Spoil Her Spa Day

Designer: Lisa Johnson

ⓐ INVITATION

1. Make card from cardstock.
2. Adhere patterned paper strip to patterned paper rectangle. Die-cut small scalloped border from patterned paper strip; adhere.
3. Ink edges of panel and tie on ribbon. Adhere to card.
4. Die-cut label from cardstock. Stamp leaves, you're invited, and just for you circle. Ink edges and adhere with foam tape.
5. Stamp "Day" on cardstock rectangle, ink edges, and adhere. Affix stickers to spell "Spa".
6. Adhere butterfly, flower, and pearl.

ⓑ FAVOR TAG

1. Die-cut small scalloped border into patterned paper, trim, and ink edges. Adhere strip to cardstock.
2. Trim panel into tag shape; ink edges.
3. Stamp name and leaf. Affix sticker.
4. Adhere ribbon. Die-cut flower from patterned paper; adhere.
5. Adhere silver flower.

ⓒ NAIL POLISH

1. Trim patterned paper to fit nail polish bottle. Ink edges and adhere.
2. Die-cut small scalloped border from patterned paper, ink edges, and adhere.
3. Adhere sequin and ribbon bow.
4. Adhere silver flower.

ⓓ BATH SALT WRAP

1. Die-cut small scalloped border from patterned paper, ink edges, and adhere to patterned paper rectangle. *Note: Ink edges of rectangle panel.*
2. Stamp bath salts on patterned paper and just for you circle on cardstock. Circle-punch and die-cut images. Ink edges and adhere to panel.
3. Adhere panel around clear tubes.

ⓔ BOTTLE WRAP

1. Die-cut small scalloped border from patterned paper, ink edges, and adhere to patterned paper rectangle. *Note: Ink edges of rectangle panel.*
2. Die-cut circle from cardstock. Stamp medium circle, leaves, and name.
3. Adhere ribbon bow. Die-cut flower from patterned paper.
4. Adhere pearl.
5. Adhere panel around bottle.

ⓕ NAIL FILE FAVOR

1. Fold patterned paper to fit around nail file. Adhere to create pocket and ink edges.
2. Die-cut small scalloped border from patterned paper. Ink edges and adhere.
3. Tie on ribbon.
4. Die-cut label from cardstock. Stamp leaves and name. Ink edges and adhere.
5. Adhere silver flower and insert nail file in pocket.

Try This

- Tie your favor tag to a tasty snack your guests can munch on while being pampered.

- Create your own bath salts by combining Epsom salt, colorant, and fragrance (like Hungarian Lavender Oil) in a bowl. Once mixed, pour it into your clear tubes.

Fortunate Chinese New Year

Designer: Teri Anderson

ⓐ INVITATION & PLACE CARDS

❶ Trim large circle from cardstock for invitation and small circles for place cards. Ink edges, fold in fourths, and adhere ends to create fortune cookie.

❷ Print text on cardstock, trim, ink edges, and insert inside fortune cookie.

ⓑ CHOPSTICKS WRAP

❶ Adhere cardstock and patterned paper strips around chopsticks.

❷ Tie on string.

ⓒ FOOD TAG

❶ Circle-punch cardstock; adhere patterned paper strips.

❷ Print text on cardstock, trim, ink edges, and adhere to circle with foam tape.

❸ Hole-punch and tie on string.

ⓓ ENVELOPE FAVOR

❶ Adhere cardstock and patterned paper strips to envelope.

❷ Print "Shine brightly" on cardstock, trim, and ink edges.

❸ Stamp dangles on panel; color with marker. Draw line.

❹ Stamp round lantern on cardstock, trim, and adhere.

❺ Adhere rhinestone to panel and adhere to envelope.

ⓔ LANTERN

❶ Trim patterned paper rectangle.

❷ Fold in half, cut lines, and adhere top and bottom together to create cylinder.

❸ Hole-punch top and tie on string.

❹ Repeat steps 1-3 using cardstock for remaining lanterns.

Try This

- Encourage your guests to write their New Year's resolutions on a slip of paper and place it in the envelope. Suggest they open the envelope the following year to see how they did.

- Serve food from white take-out boxes for a fun and easy-to-clean alternative to fancy platters.

Let's bring in Chi
Dinner
5 pm

ⓐ

Wontons

ⓔ

Shine brightly

ⓓ

Fried Rice

ⓒ

Lea

Julie

ⓐ

Kelly

Chan

ⓑ

Art Deco Celebration

Designer: Windy Robinson

(a) INVITATION

1. Make invitation from cardstock; adhere patterned paper rectangles.
2. Print "New year's party" on cardstock, trim, and adhere.
3. Adhere rhinestones and feather.
4. Tie on ribbon.

(b) GLASS TAG

1. Trim rectangle from patterned paper.
2. Circle-punch panel and trim slit.
3. Adhere cardstock rectangle to patterned paper rectangle. Adhere to tag.

(c) DANCE CARD BOOK

1. Adhere patterned paper to notebook cover.
2. Stamp sentiment on patterned paper strip; adhere.
3. Adhere rhinestones and tie on string.
4. Adhere patterned paper around pencil. Adhere feather and tie on ribbon.
5. Tie pencil to string.

(d) FAVOR BAG

1. Make bag from patterned paper, following pattern found on CD. Assemble.
2. Stamp sentiment on patterned paper rectangle; adhere.
3. Trim patterned paper with decorative-edge scissors; adhere.
4. Adhere rhinestones and tie on ribbon.

(e) FOOD PICK

1. Trim patterned paper strip with decorative-edge scissors; adhere around toothpick.
2. Adhere rhinestones.

(f) CONFETTI BAG

1. Fill plastic bag with patterned paper trimmed with decorative edge scissors.
2. Fold patterned paper strip over bag; staple.
3. Trim front flap with decorative-edge scissors.
4. Adhere patterned paper strip and rhinestones.
5. Tie on ribbon.

(g) CUP COZY

1. Trim patterned paper to finished size. *Note: Angle patterned paper to fit around cup. Adhere ends together.*
2. Mat cardstock with patterned paper; adhere.

(h) HORN

1. Adhere patterned paper into cone shape.
2. Trim patterned paper strip with decorative-edge scissors; adhere.
3. Adhere rhinestones.

(i) CENTERPIECE

1. Repeat Horn steps 1-3.
2. Tie on ribbon and affix stickers to spell "2012".

Designer Tip

Use your fringe scissors and scrap patterned paper to create quick and easy coordinating confetti.

Try This

Set out black markers so your guests can write their names on their drink tags and cup cozies.

Rockin' 2012

Designer: Sarah Martina Parker

ⓐ INVITATION

❶ Make invitation from cardstock; adhere patterned paper rectangle.

❷ Adhere doily and tie on ribbon.

❸ Stamp circle frame on patterned paper. Stamp you're invited on cardstock. Trim images and adhere together with foam tape.

❹ Die-cut circle from cardstock, affix stickers to spell "'12". Adhere to stamped panel and adhere to die cut label with foam tape.

❺ Adhere panel to invitation with foam tape. Tie on button with twine.

❻ Adhere star rhinestone and insert stick pins.

ⓑ FOOD PICK

❶ Stamp rectangle label, goodies, and from my kitchen on cardstock; trim.

❷ Trim doily and adhere panel.

❸ Adhere rhinestones and toothpick.

ⓒ RESOLUTION CARD

❶ Print "Resolution" on cardstock. Stamp rectangle journaling block and trim.

❷ Adhere panel to patterned paper rectangle; round top corners and hole-punch.

❸ Zigzag-stitch and affix stickers to spell "2012".

❹ Tie on ribbon and twine; adhere rhinestone.

ⓓ HEADBAND

❶ Die-cut numbers from patterned paper.

❷ Trim cardstock to fit behind numbers; adhere tinsel.

❸ Adhere numbers to panel with foam tape. Thread buttons with twine; adhere.

❹ Adhere topper to coiled headband.

ⓔ WALL HANGING

❶ Adhere cardstock strips together; accordion-fold.

❷ Zigzag-stitch sides. Die-cut sentiment from cardstock; adhere. Adhere chipboard flourish.

❸ Adhere patterned paper rectangle. Trim doily; adhere. Adhere tinsel.

❹ Die-cut numbers from cardstock and patterned paper; adhere. *Note: Adhere some with foam tape.*

❺ Adhere looped ribbon behind wall hanging. Tie on twine and adhere button.

❻ Adhere rhinestone star.

ⓕ BOTTLE WRAP

❶ Mat patterned paper strip with patterned paper. Adhere tinsel and adhere around bottle.

❷ Affix stickers to spell "2012".

❸ Tie on ribbon.

❹ Adhere trimmed doily.

❺ Die-cut circle and pinked circle from patterned paper and cardstock. Adhere to bottle with foam tape.

❻ Insert stick pins and adhere rhinestone.

Designer Tip

If you can't find a headband that matches your patterned paper, just spray paint one to match!

Try This

Place homemade goodies, like cookies or candy, in a white bucket filled with tissue paper. Add your food picks and give these little favors to your guests as they leave the party.

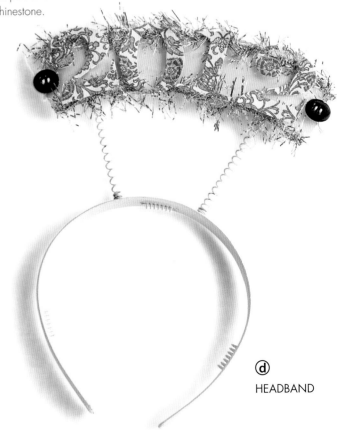

ⓓ
HEADBAND

2012

10
9
8
7
6
5
4
3
2

HAPPY NEW YEAR

2012

GOODIES FROM MY KITCHEN

GOODIES FROM MY KITCHEN

GOODIES FROM MY KITCHEN

2012 Resolution

(a)

(b)

(c)

(d)

(e)

(f)

Time Flies

Designer: Alicia Thelin

ⓐ INVITATION

❶ Make card from cardstock.
❷ Stamp clocks, hands, and time flies on cardstock rectangle. Adhere ribbon to panel and adhere to card.
❸ Tie on ribbon and adhere rhinestone.
❹ Border-punch cardstock strip; adhere.

ⓑ FAVOR BOX

❶ Die-cut box from patterned paper and cardstock; assemble.
❷ Scallop-punch cardstock; trim and adhere.
❸ Slot-punch top flaps and tie together with ribbon.

ⓒ CONFETTI POCKET

❶ Die-cut box from patterned paper. Trim and adhere to create pocket.
❷ Stamp sentiment on cardstock; circle-punch.
❸ Punch scalloped circle from cardstock, adhere circle with foam tape, and adhere panel to pocket.

ⓓ HORN

❶ Adhere patterned paper around horn.
❷ Punch scalloped circle from cardstock, trim, and adhere.

ⓔ JAR WRAP & TAG

❶ Adhere patterned paper strips together, pleat, and adhere around jar.
❷ Tie on ribbon.
❸ Stamp sentiment on cardstock; tag-punch.
❹ Border-punch cardstock, trim, and adhere to tag; staple.
❺ Punch wings from cardstock, apply glitter, and adhere to tag.
❻ Attach jump ring and thread on string.

ⓕ BANNER

❶ Stamp clocks on cardstock rectangles. Mat panels with cardstock.
❷ Die-cut "2012!" from cardstock; adhere.
❸ Insert panels into luggage tags. Attach clips.
❹ Attach eyelets to ribbon and thread on tags.

ⓖ HAT

❶ Trim and adhere patterned paper panels to create hat.
❷ Stamp clock and hands on cardstock. Trim and adhere rhinestone.
❸ Punch wings from cardstock, apply glitter, and adhere to clock. Adhere to hat with foam tape.
❹ Staple on twill and adhere looped tulle.

Try This

Right before midnight, have everyone share their favorite moment of 2011.

Vintage Valentine's Day

Designer: Melissa Phillips

(a) TREE
1. Wrap tree form in tissue garland; secure with heart and pearl pins.
2. Attach die cut tickets, heart stickers, and vintage images with pearl pins.
3. Adhere paper roses.
4. Wrap patterned paper around wooden spool and adhere. Adhere to upside-down tart tin and tree.

(b) NAPKIN RING
1. Die-cut doily from patterned paper.
2. Adhere ribbon.
3. Adhere ticket with foam tape.
4. Affix heart sticker.
5. Wrap around napkin and tie ribbon.

(c) INVITATION
1. Make card from cardstock, ink edges, and round right corners.
2. Die-cut large doily from patterned paper, ink edges, and adhere.
3. Trim patterned paper and adhere. Tie ribbon around 10 reasons tag; adhere.
4. Adhere child with foam tape.
5. Thread smitten tag and button with thread and tie to bow.

(d) TREAT BAG
1. Fill treat bag with candies.
2. Affix my valentine sticker to border sticker with foam tape. Affix with foam tape.
3. Affix heart sticker.
4. Adhere flowers.

(e) PLACE CARD
1. Fold tag in half.
2. Adhere vintage cupid.
3. Adhere rose.

(f) BANNER
1. Trim tags and adhere to doilies.
2. Adhere vintage images with foam tape.
3. Adhere doilies to ribbon.
4. Adhere hearts between doilies. Affix heart stickers.
5. Tie tulle strips.
6. Ink all tag edges, adhere letters to spell "Hugs", and adhere.
7. Adhere buttons.

(g) CUPCAKE TOPPER
1. Adhere vintage cupid to toothpick.
2. Adhere heart and flower.

Try This

Have a station for guests to create their own homemade Valentines. Provide red & pink cardstock, heart punches, doilies, scissors, and glue sticks.

Sweet Valentine's Day

Designer: Ashley Cannon Newell

ⓐ CAKE TOPPER

1. Cover chipboard birds with patterned paper.
2. Paint bird legs and beaks.
3. Die-cut large circle from cardstock. Adhere foam squares. Adhere twine to create nest.
4. Attach bird legs into foam.

ⓑ PLACEMAT

1. Stamp polka dot pattern.
2. Trim patterned paper strips and adhere.

ⓒ INVITATION

1. Make card from cardstock.
2. Emboss cardstock and die-cut into heart. Ink edges and adhere.
3. Die-cut scalloped circle from cardstock and ink edges.
4. Die-cut circle from patterned paper. Stamp you're invited and heat emboss. Adhere to scalloped circle. Adhere with foam tape.
5. Tie on ribbon and tulle. Adhere trim and flower.

ⓓ PILLOW BOX FAVOR

1. Die-cut pillow box from cardstock and die-cut circle.
2. Trim transparency sheet and adhere to create window.
3. Stamp sentiments.
4. Adhere floral trim and assemble box.
5. Stamp swirl heart and XOXO on cardstock, die-cut into heart, and ink edges.
6. Adhere heart and locket.
7. Tie on ribbon and tulle. Adhere flower.

ⓔ BANNER

1. Die-cut and emboss large and small hearts from cardstock; ink. Tie on ribbon and adhere together with foam tape.
2. Die-cut circles and scalloped circles from cardstock and ink edges. Adhere together using foam tape.
3. Stamp letter on cardstock to spell "Love", die-cut into circles, ink edges, and adhere using foam tape.
4. Tie hearts together with ribbon to create banner.

Try This

Ask guests to bring their favorite decadent sweet treat and say good-bye to the diet for just one day.

Hearts & Doilies

Designer: Maile Belles

ⓐ BANNER

1. Die-cut doilies from various cardstock.
2. Stamp be mine hearts, polka dot hearts, and solid flourish heart on cardstock. Trim and adhere with foam tape.
3. String doilies on thread.

ⓑ FAVOR BAG

1. Trim large cardstock strip; score at folds.
2. Fill cellophane bag with treats and fold down top. Fold cardstock around bag and adhere.
3. Die-cut doily from paper and stamp with love.
4. Place doily on bag and circle punch twice.
5. Thread ribbon through holes and tie bow.

ⓒ CANDLE DÉCOR

1. Die-cut lace border from cardstock.
2. Adhere to candle.
3. Tie on ribbon.

ⓓ INVITATION

1. Make card from cardstock.
2. Die-cut doily from paper and adhere.
3. Die-cut envelope from cardstock. Assemble and adhere.
4. Stamp background and rectangle border on cardstock. Stamp you're invited, oval with hearts, and parallel lines.
5. Die-cut rectangle, place in envelope, and adhere with foam tape.
6. Thread buttons with string and adhere.
7. Tie on ribbon.

ⓔ PLACE CARD

1. Die-cut two rounded frames from cardstock, score, and adhere together to create stand-up card base.
2. Die-cut doily from cardstock.
3. Stamp dotted heart border. Adhere.
4. Die-cut double ended banner from cardstock, write guest name with pen, and adhere with foam tape.
5. Thread button with ribbon and adhere.

ⓕ NAPKIN RING

1. Trim ring from paper towel roll.
2. Trim cardstock strip and adhere. Wrap with ribbon and adhere.
3. Die-cut doily from cardstock; adhere.
4. Tie bow with ribbon and adhere.

ⓖ CUPCAKE TOPPER

1. Die-cut doily from cardstock. Adhere toothpick.
2. Stamp images and sentiment on cardstock. Die-cut into circle and adhere with foam tape.

Spring Plant Exchange

Designer: Windy Robinson

ⓐ BANNER

1. Trim triangles from patterned paper.
2. Trim cardstock, ink edges, and adhere.
3. Trim patterned paper strips and adhere.
4. Die-cut scalloped circles from patterned paper and adhere.
5. Border-punch cardstock strips and adhere.
6. Adhere chipboard letters to spell "Welcome".
7. Hole-punch pennants and attach with rings.

ⓑ SEED FAVOR TINS

1. Fill tin with seeds.
2. Trim patterned paper strip, wrap tin, and adhere.
3. Wrap ribbon and tie bow.
4. Stamp thanks sentiment on cardstock, trim, and hole-punch. Tie on with twine. Attach pin.

ⓒ INVITATION

1. Make invitation from patterned paper.
2. Print text on cardstock. Mat with cardstock and adhere.
3. Tie bow with ribbon, attach pins, and adhere.
4. Make spiral rose from patterned paper and adhere.

ⓓ LABEL FRAMES

1. Print sentiment on cardstock, trim, and place in frame.
2. Cover frame with patterned paper and sand edges.
3. Trim large triangles from assorted patterned paper. Border-punch cardstock strips and adhere to triangles. Adhere.
4. Tie bows with twine and adhere. Attach pins.
5. Make spiral rose from cardstock and adhere.

ⓔ PLANT ID TAG

1. Place tissue paper in clay pot.
2. Print label on cardstock. Mat with patterned paper and cardstock.
3. Adhere to snack pins and place in pot.

ⓕ BUCKET

1. Trim triangles from assorted patterned paper.
2. Border-punch cardstock strips and adhere to triangles.
3. Stitch together to create banner. Adhere.
4. Tie on ribbon.
5. Print guest name on cardstock, hole-punch, and adhere patterned paper strip. Tie on with twine.

ⓖ PENNANT

1. Make pennant from patterned paper.
2. Border-punch cardstock strip and adhere.
3. Trim patterned paper strip and adhere.
4. Wrap with ribbon, tie bow, and attach pins.
5. Make spiral rose from patterned paper and adhere.
6. Stamp flowers bloom sentiment on cardstock, trim, and hole-punch. Thread with twine and tie on.
7. Adhere to dowel and place in bucket.

ⓗ FLOWER

1. Make spiral rose from cardstock and adhere to dowel.
2. Tie on ribbon and attach pin.
3. Stamp kindness sentiment on cardstock, hole-punch, and tie on with twine.
4. Place in bucket.

ⓘ PINWHEEL

1. Make pinwheel from patterned paper and adhere to dowel.
2. Tie bow with ribbon and adhere.
3. Stamp your friends sentiment on cardstock, hole-punch, and tie on with twine.
4. Make spiral rose from cardstock and adhere.
5. Place in bucket.

Designer Tip

Invitation and plant ID tag wording can be found on included CD.

Try This

Have a clay pot filled with seed packets by the door for guests to take as they leave.

Come to a
Garden Party
Join me at my home on
May 2, 2011
1:00 - 3:00 pm

If you are a gardener, bring a plant from
your garden to share. If new to gardening
bring your favorite summer hors d'oeuvre
and recipe to share. All should come ready
to take home some new plants to love.

Plants

Food

Shelly

Cute Easter Party

Designer: Chan Vuong

ⓐ INVITATION

1. Die-cut label from cardstock.
2. Trim invitation from patterned paper, round corners, and punch slot.
3. Thread ribbon and adhere to label with foam tape.
4. Stamp train on cardstock, color, and trim. Adhere with foam tape.

ⓑ THANK YOU CARD

1. Make card from cardstock, cover with patterned paper, and round corners.
2. Die-cut label from cardstock, stamp sheep on hill and thank ewe, and color.
3. Affix banner sticker and adhere with foam tape.

ⓒ ENVELOPE

1. Die-cut envelope from cardstock, assemble, and adhere.
2. Trim journal card from patterned paper, round corners, and adhere.
3. Affix sticker.

ⓓ PLACEMAT

1. Die-cut place mat from patterned paper.
2. Die-cut large label from patterned paper and adhere.
3. Affix banner.

ⓔ PLACE CARD

1. Make card from cardstock, cover with patterned paper, and round corners.
2. Trim label from cardstock and adhere.
3. Affix stickers to spell guest name.
4. Stamp carrot car bunny on cardstock, color, and trim. Adhere with foam tape.

ⓕ FAVOR BOX

1. Trim patterned paper strip and adhere to box.
2. Trim ribbon and adhere.
3. Die-cut scalloped circle from patterned paper.
4. Stamp circle sentiment and chick on cardstock, color, and punch into circle.
5. Adhere to scalloped circle and adhere with foam tape.

ⓖ BASKET

1. Die-cut basket and handle from cardstock.
2. Assemble and adhere.
3. Affix lace banner stickers.

ⓗ CUPCAKE TOPPER

1. Stamp banner and egg on cardstock.
2. Color, trim, and adhere together.
3. Adhere to lollipop stick.

ⓘ CUPCAKE STANDS

1. Stamp cupcake stand pieces with polka dot background.
2. Assemble stands.

Designer Tip

When there are exposed parts of stickers, such as the banners hanging off of the Easter basket in this case, affix exposed parts to cardstock and trim.

happy easter

PARTY

TO
FROM
WHEN
WHERE

Thank Ewe!

LOU

on Easter tweet for you

Sacred Easter Celebration

Designer: Renae Curtz

ⓐ EGG CUP

1. Die-cut scalloped square from cardstock.
2. Score, trim, and adhere sides to form box.
3. Stamp cardstock strip with blossom branches; adhere.
4. Stamp butterfly on cardstock, trim, and adhere pearl. Adhere with foam tape.
5. Place egg in cup.

ⓑ CARD

1. Make card from cardstock.
2. Stamp sentiment.
3. Border-punch cardstock strip and adhere to cardstock. Stitch and apply rub-on. Stamp branch. Adhere.
4. Trim cross from cardstock. Adhere sticker to cross with foam tape.
5. Adhere rhinestone and adhere cross with foam tape.

ⓒ FLOWER

1. Using template from flower kit, trim petals and leaves from cardstock.
2. Assemble as directed in flower kit instructions.

ⓓ BASKET

1. Score and fold cardstock to create box. Stamp branch and adhere sides.
2. Trim strip of cardstock and attach with brads.
3. Stamp butterfly on cardstock, trim, and adhere pearl. Adhere with foam tape.
4. Fill with paper shreds.
5. Place candy in bags, tie with ribbon, and place in basket.

ⓔ MENU

1. Print menu on cardstock, stamp blossom branch, and trim.
2. Mat with cardstock.
3. Stamp blossom branches on cardstock, trim, and border-punch. Stitch top edge and adhere.
4. Stamp butterfly on cardstock, trim, and adhere pearl. Adhere with foam tape.

Try This

Invite everyone to a lovely brunch after attending the Easter Sunrise Service together.

JOY behold GOD everything

Easter wishes

ⓑ

Easter Brunch Menu

Mimosa

Broiled Grapefruit

Eggs Benedict

Roasted Asparagus

Shallot Butter

Berry Trifle

ⓓ

ⓔ

ⓒ

ⓐ

Mother's Day Tea Party

Designer: Melissa Phillips

ⓐ CENTERPIECE

1. Fill teacup with foam block and paper shreds; adhere flowers.
2. Adhere pearls to mother label.
3. Wrap popsicle stick with ribbon; adhere.
4. Tie on ribbon, tie bow, and adhere flower.
5. Insert popsicle stick into foam.
6. Place teacup on tea saucer.

ⓑ PLACE CARD

1. Ink envelope edges.
2. Trim strip of patterned paper and adhere.
3. Stamp take time for tea on cardstock, die-cut into banner, and ink edges. Adhere.
4. Tie on ribbon and tie bow.
5. Print vintage teacup with hearts on cardstock, trim, and ink edges.
5. Affix stickers to spell name.
6. Insert card into envelope.

ⓒ INVITATION

1. Make card from cardstock.
2. Adhere patterned paper rectangles. Stitch edges.
3. Trim slit, thread ribbon, and tie bow. Adhere flower.
4. Print vintage strawberry cake on cardstock, trim, and ink edges. Stamp tea time and tea kettle and adhere with foam tape.
5. Stamp sentiment on cardstock, die-cut into banner, and ink edges. Adhere.
6. Thread buttons with twine and adhere.

ⓓ NAPKIN RING

1. Trim strip of patterned paper, adhere ends, and insert fabric.
2. Wrap ribbon and tie bow.
3. Print vintage ticket on cardstock, trim, and hole-punch.
4. Thread button and ticket with twine and tie on.

ⓔ FAVOR BAG

1. Adhere patterned paper to bag.
2. Trim patterned paper strip and adhere.
3. Print vintage chocolate cake on cardstock, trim, and ink edges. Adhere.
4. Adhere doily. Adhere velvet leaf and flower.

ⓕ CUPCAKE PICK

1. Die-cut doily from patterned paper; adhere trim.
2. Adhere food pick.
3. Die-cut scalloped square from patterned paper. Adhere with foam tape.
4. Print vintage cupcake on patterned paper, trim, and adhere with foam tape.

Try This

Give mom a seat of honor and take turns letting everyone serve her.

Afternoon Tea for Mom

Designer: Latisha Yoast

ⓐ SANDWICH PICK

1. Die-cut large label from patterned paper. Trim skewer and adhere.
2. Die-cut small label from patterned paper.
3. Stamp name of sandwich and adhere with foam tape.
4. Tie on ribbon.

ⓑ TEA POUCH

1. Trim large rectangle of patterned paper. Die-cut label from each end.
2. Score, fold, and assemble pouch. Adhere.
3. Stamp sentiment on patterned paper, trim, and adhere.
4. Adhere flower.
5. Insert tea bag into pouch.

ⓒ TEA CUP NAME TAG

1. Die-cut small label from patterned paper.
2. Stamp guest name.
3. Hole-punch and thread with twine.
4. Adhere flower.

ⓓ NAPKIN RING

1. Trim strip of patterned paper and border-punch. Adhere ends together to form ring.
2. Wrap with ribbon and adhere.
3. Affix sticker.

ⓔ CARD

1. Make card from cardstock.
2. Trim strip of patterned paper and mat with patterned paper. Adhere.
3. Stamp "Happy mother's day" and adhere rhinestones.
4. Tie ribbon around dried flowers and adhere.

ⓕ BASKET

1. Die-cut doily from patterned paper.
2. Trim strip of patterned paper and adhere to doily.

ⓖ TIN

1. Trim strip of patterned paper and mat with patterned paper.
2. Wrap around tin and adhere ends together.
3. Wrap ribbon and tie bow.
4. Die-cut label from patterned paper, ink edges, and stamp sentiment.
5. Adhere fabric flower and adhere with foam tape.

ⓗ GLASS TEA JAR

1. Fill glass jar with loose leaf tea.
2. Tie rhinestone charm to jar with twine.
3. Die-cut label from patterned paper and stamp herbal tea circle.
4. Adhere with foam tape.

Designer Tip

It is easy to create custom sandwich and food picks when using your favorite alphabet stamps, rather than printing or finding stamp sets that contain those words.

Try This

Find out what your guest of honor's favorite tea is and put it in the tea jar.

tuna

chicken

egg

Happy Mother's Day

SPECIAL FRIEND
blend

STEEP, STIR & *enjoy*

HERBAL
TEA
COMPANY

Mom

Country Mother's Day

Designer: Joannie McBride

(a) GIFT BOX

1. Trim wrapping paper and wrap box.
2. Tie on ribbon.
3. Punch circles from patterned paper. Adhere together with foam tape. Adhere
4. Write "Love" on cardstock, trim into tag, and adhere.
5. Thread button with twine and adhere.

(b) CARD

1. Make card from cardstock.
2. Adhere cardstock and patterned paper rectangles.
3. Punch circles from patterned paper and cardstock. Layer and adhere to card with foam tape. *Note: Crumple some circles before adhering.*
4. Thread button with twine and adhere. Adhere ribbon.
5. Affix stickers to spell "Happy mother's day".

(c) BANNER

1. Ink edges of banner triangles.
2. Trim long piece of ribbon and staple triangles. Tie knots on ribbon ends.
3. Punch circles from cardstock and patterned paper. Adhere together and adhere to banner. Thread buttons with twine and adhere.
4. Affix stickers to spell "Mother".
5. Punch small scalloped circles from patterned paper. Attach with brad.
6. Staple triangles and flowers to ribbon.

(d) MASON JAR

1. Trim wrapping paper and place under lid.
2. Adhere ribbon to lid.
3. Punch circle and scalloped circle from patterned paper. Attach with brad and adhere.
4. Trim wrapping paper to fit lid top and attach lid.
5. Thread tag with twine and tie on.

(e) CUPCAKE PICK

1. Punch circles and scalloped circles from assorted patterned paper and cardstock.
2. Adhere together.
3. Attach brad or thread button and adhere.
4. Trim skewer and adhere to flower.
5. Punch scalloped circle and adhere to back.

(f) FLOWER POT

1. Trim wrapping paper and adhere to pot. Trim slits.
2. Place foam cylinder in pot. Cover with paper shred.
3. Wrap ribbon around pot and adhere.
4. Punch circle and scalloped circle from cardstock and patterned paper. Adhere together and adhere to pot. Thread button with twine and adhere.
5. Punch large scalloped circle from cardstock and punch small circle from patterned paper. Adhere together. Thread button with twine and adhere or attach brad.
6. Adhere to skewer. Insert into foam.

Try This

Set up everything on the front porch and have rockers available, especially one for the guest of honor.

Retro TV Father's Day

Designer: Heidi Van Laar

ⓐ TREAT BAG

1. Make treat bag from patterned paper, following pattern found on CD.
2. Score sides and flap and adhere side and bottom.
3. Trim patterned paper, round bottom corners, and mat with cardstock. Round bottom corners.
4. Trim and adhere ribbon to panel and adhere panel to flap.
5. Die-cut circle from cardstock, mat with cardstock, and adhere.
6. Stamp TV on circle, cardstock, and assorted patterned paper. Paper-piece and adhere to circle panel with foam tape.
7. Color with marker.

ⓑ SODA BOTTLE WRAP

Note: This wrap fits around a 16 oz. soda bottle.

1. Trim patterned paper.
2. Stamp TV's randomly over circles.
3. Wrap around bottle and adhere.
4. Trim patterned paper, wrap around bottle-neck, and adhere.
5. Trim ribbon and adhere.
6. Die-cut circle from patterned paper and mat with cardstock circle.
7. Affix stickers to spell "Pop" and adhere.

ⓒ CARD

1. Make card from cardstock. Cover with patterned paper.
2. Trim patterned paper and adhere. Trim patterned paper strip and adhere with foam tape.
3. Die-cut patterned paper circle and adhere with foam tape.
4. Trim ribbon and adhere.
5. Die-cut cardstock circle, stamp TV, and adhere with foam tape.
6. Stamp TV on cardstock and assorted patterned paper, trim, and paper-piece. Adhere with foam tape. Color with marker.
7. Stamp dad on patterned paper, trim, and adhere.

ⓓ CARD SHEETS

1. Print title and lines on cardstock. Trim and mat with patterned paper.
2. Die-cut circle from patterned paper and adhere.
3. Stamp TV on cardstock and patterned paper, trim, and paper-piece.
4. Stamp dad, color with marker, and adhere with foam tape.

ⓔ NAPKIN RING

1. Trim strip of patterned paper, adhere ends together, and adhere ribbon.
2. Trim ribbon and adhere.
3. Die-cut circles from cardstock and patterned paper; adhere together.
4. Stamp TV on cardstock and assorted patterned paper, trim, and paper-piece.
5. Color with marker and adhere with foam tape.

ⓕ FOOD PICK

1. Stamp TV on cardstock and assorted patterned paper, trim, and paper-piece.
2. Color with marker.
3. Print sentiment on patterned paper, trim, and adhere.
4. Adhere to skewers.
5. Stamp TV on patterned paper, trim, and adhere to back with foam tape.

ⓖ CENTERPIECE

1. Die-cut circles from patterned paper and cardstock, adhere together, and affix stickers to spell sentiment.
2. Trim large circle from patterned paper, cut in half, and adhere skewers to one half. Adhere other half to backside with foam tape.
3. Adhere letter circles to spell sentiment.
4. Die-cut circles from cardstock and adhere to backsides of letter circles.
5. Die-cut circles from cardstock, adhere together, and stamp TV.

6. Stamp TV on cardstock and assorted patterned paper, trim, and paper-piece. Adhere with foam tape.
7. Color with marker. Adhere panel using foam tape.
8. Trim wedges of cardstock and adhere to back to prop up centerpiece.

ⓗ FRAME

1. Paint frame.
2. Cover with patterned paper and trim opening slightly larger than frame opening.
3. Use marker to accent edges and draw center details.
4. Die-cut circles from cardstock, adhere to discs, and adhere.
5. Trim large circle from cardstock and adhere to frame back.
6. Color craft sticks with marker and adhere.
7. Die-cut circles from cardstock and sandwich craft sticks by adhering together with foam tape.
8. Die-cut large circle from cardstock and adhere to backside of antennae bottom.

Designer Tips

- When adhering paper to the skewers, use a piece of foam tape on either side of the skewer. The foam tape acts as a spacer and makes the adhesion more sturdy.

- Template for the card sheets can be found on included CD.

Try This

Use the card sheets to have party attendees write down some of their favorite things about the man being celebrated. After the party, the sheets can be bound together to create a wonderful keepsake for Dad.

This Beer's for You, Dad!

Designer: Sarah Jay

ⓐ INVITATION
1. Stamp cardstock with zigzag background; trim.
2. Print digital element and invitation text on cardstock and adhere.

ⓑ TASTING PLACEMAT
1. Print numbers, circles, and "this beer's for" on cardstock.
2. Mask circles and stamp zigzag background.
3. Remove masks and adhere panel to cardstock.
4. Write name of guest with pen.

ⓒ MENU
1. Print digital element and menu text on cardstock.
2. Trim and place in sign holder.

ⓓ SIGN
1. Print digital element and sentiment on cardstock.
2. Place in frame.

ⓔ NOTEBOOK
1. Adhere cardstock to front of notebook.
2. Stamp zigzag background.
3. Print "Tasting notes" on cardstock. Stamp large border and die-cut into label. Affix beer glass sticker and adhere.

ⓕ FOOD LABEL
1. Print food name on cardstock.
2. Stamp small border and die-cut label.
3. Stamp zigzag background.
4. Push memo pin into bottle cap. Secure with foam tape on underside.
5. Slide label into memo pin.

ⓖ BOTTLE WRAP
1. Make label from paper.
2. Stamp zigzag border on cardstock, trim, and adhere.
3. Stamp narrow label on cardstock and die-cut. Trim and adhere.
4. Print digital element on cardstock and die-cut number. Adhere with foam tape.
5. Adhere ends of wrap and adhere to bottle.

Designer Tips
- If you don't have a chevron or zigzag stamp available, use a plaid or geometric background stamp.

- Templates for the menu, invitation, tasting placemat, and sign can be found on included CD.

Try This
- Organize your tasting from lightest to darkest to get the most out of each beer.

- Not a beer drinker? Try organizing a tasting with scotch or gourmet sodas instead.

d

e

tasting
NOTES

DAD
This Beer's
FOR YOU

g

4   1
2   6

b

Sliders
with Caramelized Onions
and Chipotle Mayo

f

Homemade
Pretzels

Dark Chocolate
Truffles

Please join us for a
Father's Day
BEER TASTING PARTY

Enjoy six brews,
good friends,
and great food.

Saturday, June 25 at 8pm
12 Porter Road - Boston

RSVP to 555-123-6789

please drink responsibly.

a

c

Beer List & Appetizers

Hoegarden .... Hummus

Victory Prima Pils .... Thai Spring Rolls

Sierra Nevada Pale Ale .... Homemade Pretzels

Dogfish Head 90 Minute IPA .... Mini Crab Cakes w/ Lemon

Alaskan Smoked Porter .... Sliders w/ Caramelized Onions

Bells Expedition Stout .... Dark Chocolate Truffles

Summer Picnic

Designer: Melissa Phillips

ⓐ INVITATION

Ink all edges.

❶ Fold up bottom of bag and trim edge with decorative-edge scissors.
❷ Trim and adhere patterned paper strip.
❸ Trim and adhere patterned paper block. Stitch three edges.
❹ Dye trim with shimmer spray; adhere.
❺ Spray shimmer spray on recipe card; affix border strip and insert in pocket.
❻ Trim seed packet from patterned paper; stamp sentiment, distress edges, and adhere.
❼ Tie on ribbon.
❽ Stamp strawberries on tag; color with markers. Thread twine through button and tag; tie to ribbon.

See inside image of invitation on p. 283

ⓑ FAVOR BAG

❶ Fill bag. Cut burlap strip and adhere.
❷ Trim seed packet from patterned paper; distress edges and adhere.
❸ Tie on ribbon.
❹ Affix border stickers.

ⓒ JAR

❶ Trim and adhere patterned paper strip to jar.
❷ Trim jar image from patterned paper; stamp garden fresh and adhere.
❹ Adhere chipboard button; affix sticker.
❺ Trim burlap and tie on with twine.
❻ Repeat step 8 from Invitation.

ⓓ FOOD PICK

❶ Die-cut banner from patterned paper; fold.
❷ Trim seed packet from patterned paper and staple to banner.
❸ Adhere to toothpick.
❹ Distress button, thread with twine, and adhere.

ⓔ NAPKIN RING

❶ Trim patterned paper strip; staple ends.
❷ Adhere flower.
❸ Trim and adhere burlap.
❹ Affix sentiment.
❺ Thread button with twine and adhere.

Designer Tip

Write party details on recipe card for a clever homespun invitation.

Try This

Provide terra cotta pots and seeds or flats of annuals for guests to create their own flower or vegetable creations to take home.

Vintage Soda Shop

Designer: Betsy Veldman

ⓐ CHALKBOARD

1. Trim and adhere patterned paper to chalkboard frame. Sand edges.
2. Affix sticker.

ⓑ STRAW

1. Die-cut circles from patterned paper.
2. Adhere bottle caps.
3. Punch watermelons from patterned paper and adhere.
4. Affix stickers.
5. Punch holes and slip on straws.

ⓒ SKEWER

1. Punch watermelons from patterned paper; adhere to both sides of skewer.
2. Punch strawberry from patterned paper; adhere with foam tape.
3. Tie on twill.

ⓓ BOTTLE WRAP

1. Using pattern on included CD, trim and adhere patterned paper.
2. Die-cut label from cardstock; stamp label and adhere.
3. Die-cut circle from patterned paper; stamp 5 cents, mat with patterned paper, and adhere.
4. Repeat step 2 from Skewer.
5. Punch watermelon from patterned paper; adhere to bottle cap.

ⓔ COASTER

1. Cut patterned paper circle to fit inside bottle cap; adhere.

ⓕ BUCKET DECORATION

1. Repeat step 1 from Coaster.
2. Adhere to bucket.

ⓖ INVITATION

1. Cut bottle base from cardstock, following pattern found on CD.
2. Cut two pieces from patterned paper following bottle liquid pattern; adhere.
3. Cut two pieces from cardstock following bottle cap pattern: adhere. Add details with pen.
4. Print sentiment on cardstock; adhere.
5. Print text on patterned paper; adhere.
6. Trim and adhere patterned paper strips.
7. Affix girl sticker.

Designer Tip

Seal coasters with decoupage medium if waterproofing is desired.

Try This

- Set up an ice cream bar and let partygoers create their own floats. Serve ice cream in old fashioned soda dishes.

- Encourage guests to dress in 50's attire like poodle skirts, bowling shirts, and bobby socks.

Join us for some *old-fashioned* fun!
Where: Our Backyard
When: August 11, 6:00pm

ⓖ
INVITATION

End of the School Year

Designer: Jennifer McGuire

(a) INVITATION

1. Make card from cardstock.
2. Stamp alphabet repeatedly along edges.
3. Print text on cardstock; mat with cardstock and adhere.
4. Stamp dashed line.
5. Stamp bus on cardstock; color with markers and cut out.
6. Print "school's out!" on cardstock; trim and cut into banner.
7. Adhere floss between bus and banner; adhere with foam tape.

(b) NOTEBOOK

1. Trim cardstock and adhere to notebook.
2. Repeat steps 2-3 from Invitation.
3. Print pencils on cardstock; color with markers, cut out, and adhere.

(c) FAVOR BAG

1. Trim cardstock and adhere to bag.
2. Repeat steps 2-7 from Invitation.

(d) STRAW

1. Punch circle from cardstock; punch dashed lines. Mat with cardstock.
2. Print "School's out" on cardstock; trim and adhere.
3. Stamp schoolhouse; color with markers and adhere.
4. Adhere to straw.

(e) BINGO CARD

1. Download bingo card found on CD. Type names and print on cardstock.
2. Mat with cardstock.

(f) COLORING CARD

1. Print "Color Me!" on cardstock; trim.
2. Stamp pencil on cardstock; color with markers, cut out, and adhere.
3. Stamp animal on cardstock; trim.
4. Insert cards in ziptop bag.

Designer Tips

- If you don't have enough paper for a full mat, just use cardstock strips.

- Use buttons for bingo pieces.

Try This

Gather at the park with frisbees, bubbles, and kickball for the kids to burn off their end of the school year excitement.

Summer Fun!

Designer: Davinie Fiero

ⓐ INVITATION

1. Make card from cardstock.
2. Trim patterned paper; punch one edge. Wrap on twine and adhere. Stitch three edges.
3. Punch circles from patterned paper; mat with punched cardstock circles. Trim and adhere.
4. Ink letters and affix to spell "Summer Fun".
5. Thread button with twine and adhere.

ⓑ GARLAND

1. Repeat step 3 from Invitation; stitch together.
2. Spray flowers with shimmer spray; tie on to garland.

ⓒ NAPKIN RING

1. Trim patterned paper strips; adhere ends.

ⓓ JAR GARLAND

1. Repeat step 1 from Garland.
2. Tie around jar.

ⓔ DRINK UMBRELLA

1. Punch circle from patterned paper; cut out wedge, fold over, and adhere.
2. Adhere to skewer.

ⓕ TABLE RUNNER

1. Trim three pieces of patterned paper to 8" x 12"; adhere to create strip.
2. Repeat step 3 from Invitation; align on edges and stitch.

Try This

- Serve summer salads, barbecued chicken, and popsicles for a light, refreshing meal.

- Provide butterfly nets and jars with pierced lids for catching crickets and other fun insects.

Summer Fun

Ice Cream Social

Designer: Cristina Kowalczyk

(a) INVITATION

1. Print text on cardstock; color with markers.
2. Stamp banners.
3. Stamp ice cream cone; color edge with marker.
4. Mat with patterned paper.

(b) MENU

1. Repeat steps 1-2 from Invitation.
2. Adhere to pennant; trim excess.
3. Trim and adhere patterned paper.

(c) BANNER

1. Trim and adhere cardstock to pennants.
2. Die-cut patterned paper circles; trim and adhere.
3. Print letters on patterned paper to spell "YUM". Cut out and adhere.
4. Punch holes and thread twine through to connect pennants.

(d) FLAVOR PICK

1. Punch scalloped circle from patterned paper; die-cut circle from patterned paper. Adhere on either side of skewer with foam tape.
2. Print flavor on cardstock; color with markers. Die-cut into banner and adhere.

(e) CONE WRAP

1. Cut cone from paper, using pattern found on CD.
2. Trim and adhere patterned paper strip.
3. Stamp ice cream cone.

Designer Tips

- Use computer paper, not cardstock, for cone wraps. It's more flexible.

- Invitation and menu can be found on included CD.

Try This

- Have your party outside to accommodate drips and melting. Lay a large cloth under your display to catch messes.

- Provide toppings for the ice cream. Create wraps or labels to match the theme.

VANILLA

CHOCOLATE

BUTTER PECAN

MENU

Ice Creams
Vanilla
Chocolate
Butter Pecan

Toppings
Sprinkles
Marshmallows
M&Ms

Other
Fun
Full tummies
Good times

Join us for an
old-fashioned

ICE CREAM
SOCIAL

12 Lincoln St.
Saturday, June 12
at 3 p.m.

Beat the Heat

Designer: Joannie McBride

(a) BANNER

1. Cut swim trunks, sun rays, and sailboat from cardstock and patterned paper, following patterns found on CD. Mat sailboats and trunks with cardstock.
2. Cut pennants from patterned paper; punch circles from cardstock.
3. Assemble suns; crinkle rays. Adhere twine in concentric circle.
4. Punch holes in trunks; thread with twine.
5. Trim patterned paper strips; adhere to sailboats.
6. Punch circles from patterned paper; mat with cardstock circle and patterned paper; trim and adhere patterned paper words. Adhere with foam tape.
7. Thread buttons with string and adhere.
8. Adhere pieces to twine. Tie on ribbons and attach clothespins.

(b) PHOTO ALBUM

1. Adhere ribbon.
2. Repeat step 6 from Banner.
3. Punch circle and cut rays from cardstock. Repeat step 3 from Banner.
4. Cut pennants, trunks, and ribbons from patterned paper; adhere to twine. Adhere to album with foam tape.
5. Adhere string to trunks. Repeat step 7 from Banner.

(c) FAVOR BAG

1. Repeat steps 1-3 from Photo Album.
2. Cut pennants from patterned paper; adhere pennants and sun to twine. Adhere to bag.
3. Repeat step 7 from Banner.

(d) INVITATION

1. Trim patterned paper; double mat with cardstock.
2. Adhere twine.
3. Repeat step 6 from Banner.
4. Repeat step 3 from Photo Album.
5. Affix stickers to spell sentiment.
6. Repeat step 7 from Banner.

(e) FOOD PICKS

1. Punch circles from patterned paper; adhere cardstock circles.
2. Punch and adhere patterned paper circles. Trim and adhere patterned paper pennant.
3. Trim and adhere patterned paper strip and patterned paper words.
4. Repeat step 7 from Banner.
5. Adhere to toothpicks.

(f) WATER BOTTLE

1. Trim and adhere cardstock strip.
2. Repeat step 6 from Banner. *Note: Do not use foam tape.*
3. Tie on twine.

Try This

- Use small plastic pails for treat containers.

- If you live near a beach, host your shindig there! If not, sprinklers and a Slip n' Slide are always fun. Make a sand castle in the sand box.

Patriotic Block Party

Designer: Kim Kesti

ⓐ INVITATION

1. Make card from cardstock.
2. Trim and adhere cardstock.
3. Stamp bikes on cardstock; trim and adhere patterned paper strip. Adhere ribbon; adhere panel to card.
4. Tie on twine.
5. Print sentiment on cardstock. Trim into banner.
6. Attach brad and adhere with foam tape.

ⓑ MENU

1. Make panel from cardstock.
2. Trim and adhere cardstock.
3. Print text on cardstock; trim and adhere patterned paper strip. Adhere.
4. Punch circle from patterned paper and adhere.
5. Punch star from cardstock; mat with cardstock and adhere with foam tape.

ⓒ PLACEMAT

1. Make placemat from cardstock.
2. Trim and adhere patterned paper strips.
3. Download and print flag image found on CD. Mat with cardstock and adhere.
4. Loop and adhere ribbon.
5. Stamp circle on cardstock; punch, write name with pen, and adhere.

ⓓ CRAYON BOX

1. Make box from cardstock following pattern found on included disk.
2. Adhere ribbon.

ⓔ STRAWS

1. Punch stars from cardstock.
2. Cut slits and slide onto straws.
3. Adhere punched stars.

ⓕ PINWHEELS

1. Trim patterned paper to 5" squares.
2. Mark center and cut from each corner almost to center.
3. Punch circles from cardstock.
4. Pull corners to center; insert pin through circles and corners and into pencil eraser. Bend back pin.

ⓖ BICYCLE RIBBONS and FAVOR BAG

1. Trim cardstock strips.
2. Staple ribbons.
3. Punch stars from cardstock; mat with cardstock and adhere.
4. Put favors in bag; trim cardstock, fold over top, and adhere.
5. Tie on twine.
6. Stamp bicycle on cardstock; punch circle; mat with punched scalloped circle and adhere with foam tape.

Designer Tips

- Use buttons on the back of the pinwheels between the paper and the pencils for stability.

- American flag coloring page can be found on included CD.

Try This

- Have a parade with bikes, trikes, and even wagons. Kids love parades!

- Serve drinks in old glass jars of various sizes. It looks cool and is a great way to recycle.

- Host a potluck supper and invite your neighbors to bring their favorite picnic dish.

Menu

BBQ Pork on a Bun
Hot Dogs
Zesty Slaw
Potluck Beans
Fruit Kabobs
Lemonade
Ice Cream Treats

STOP join our parade!
(And neighborhood block party, too)

Jack

A Festive 4th of July

Designer: Courtesy of Canvas Corp.

ⓐ BANNER

See instructions and detailed image on page 284.

ⓑ CUPCAKE WRAPPER

Ink all edges.
1. Die-cut cupcake wrapper from patterned paper and cardstock.
2. Assemble.

ⓒ CUPCAKE STAND and TOPPER

Ink all edges.
1. Punch circles from cardstock.
2. Trim patterned paper to fit stand layers; mat with circles and adhere.
3. Trim patterned paper and adhere to stand support pieces.
4. Die-cut stars from cardstock; adhere.
5. Assemble stand.
6. Trim and adhere patterned paper to cardboard tube; insert floral foam.
7. Wrap floral wires with chenille; insert into tube.
8. Cut stars from patterned paper; adhere to canvas stars. Adhere to chenille stems.
9. Tie on ribbons.
10. Punch circle from cardstock; mat with punched cardstock circle. Adhere.
11. Adhere rhinestones.
12. Fill tube with gift shred.

ⓓ WAGON CENTERPIECE

Ink all paper edges.
1. Adhere floral foam inside wagon.
2. Trim and adhere patterned paper to cardboard tubes; insert floral foam.
3. Adhere cardstock and patterned paper strips.
4. Die-cut stars from patterned paper; mat one on punched cardstock circle and adhere. Adhere rhinestones. Layer one on canvas star, mat with cardstock, and adhere.
5. Die-cut letters from cardstock to spell "USA" and adhere. Adhere rope and fray ends.
6. Adhere tubes.
7. Adhere potted silk geraniums.
8. Repeat steps 7-10 from Cupcake Stand and Topper. *Note: Save two stars.*
9. Bunch mesh and adhere to floral wires; loop ribbon and adhere to floral wires. Adhere.
10. Wrap floral wires with chenille.
11. Cut pennants from patterned paper; adhere to chenille stems. Punch holes and thread with ribbon.
12. Die-cut letters from cardstock to spell "Boom", "Bang", and "4th of July". Adhere.
13. Tie on ribbons.
14. Adhere pennants and leftover stars.
15. Fill tubes and cover wagon with gift shred.

ⓔ BOTTLE WRAP

1. Using pattern included on CD, trim patterned paper and ink edges.
2. Punch stars from cardstock; adhere and draw stitches with pen.
3. Adhere rhinestones and nailheads.
4. Adhere ends.

ⓕ BOW DECORATION

See instructions and detailed image on page 284.

ⓖ TABLE RUNNER

1. Cut canvas sheet to make banner.
2. Hem all edges with heat-activated adhesive.
3. Paint stripes.
4. Trim denim strips. Cut slits at points and thread strip through; tie around sections of rope. Unravel ends. Tie on denim strips; adhere rhinestones.
5. Cut denim stars; mat with burlap, canvas, and patterned paper stars. Adhere.
6. Adhere rhinestones.

ⓗ INVITATION

Ink all edges.
1. Print text on cardstock; mat with cardstock.
2. Hand cut patterned paper strips. Adhere in frame shape with foam tape.
3. Adhere rickrack.
4. Punch stars and starbursts from patterned paper and cardstock. Adhere with foam tape.
5. Trim sentiments from patterned paper and adhere with foam tape.
6. Adhere cork circles and rhinestones.

Designer Tips

- Adhere flag strips on banner in a wave pattern to give it dimension and interest.
- A hot glue gun works best to adhere oddly-shaped items.

Celebrate the 4th

Designer: Laura O'Donnell

ⓐ BANNER

1. Create project in software.
2. Open banner letters; resize.
3. Print twice on matte paper.
4. Cut out one set. Trim edge from second set; adhere with foam tape.
5. Punch holes and thread with twine.
6. Adhere bow and ribbon accents.

ⓑ INVITATION

1. Make card from cardstock; round corners.
2. Create project in software. Type "Let's celebrate" on journaling block. Print on matte paper, round corners, and adhere.
3. Print firecrackers on matte paper; cut out and adhere with foam tape.

ⓒ FOOD PICKS

1. Punch circles from cardstock. Adhere to fronts and backs of toothpicks.
2. Create project in software; open star, All American, and 100% elements; resize. Print on matte paper, trim, and adhere.
3. Apply glitter glue.

ⓓ NAPKIN RING

1. Create project in software. Open firecrackers; resize and copy. Print on matte paper and trim.
2. Open circle frame; resize and print on matte paper.
3. Cut out and distress edges; adhere.
4. Punch star from cardstock; adhere.
5. Adhere ends.

ⓔ CENTERPIECE

1. Trim styrofoam and insert in bucket.
2. Create project in software. Open All American element; resize and print on matte paper.
3. Double mat with cardstock. Apply glitter glue. Adhere to dowel and insert in styrofoam.
4. Add gift shred.
5. Punch stars from cardstock. Adhere one to bucket with foam tape; place others in shred.

Designer Tips

- Adhere ribbon accents to the banner by slipping twine between the accent and a small cardstock circle.

- Make back mat of centerpiece sentiment into a card shape and fold over the dowel for easier adherence.

Try This

Enhance your party décor with additional red, white, and blue supplies. You'll be able to use them year after year.

Spooktacular Soiree

Designer: Emily Branch

ⓐ BANNER

1. Die-cut pennants from patterned paper; adhere to chipboard pennants. Ink edges and punch holes.
2. Trim patterned paper strips and adhere.
3. Adhere doily and ribbon strip. Tie ribbon bow and adhere.
4. Affix stickers. *Note: Use foam tape to adhere some stickers.*
5. Adhere tinsel. Thread ribbon through pennants to form banner.
6. Thread buttons with twine and adhere. Adhere rhinestones.

ⓑ CANDY CONE

1. Make cone from patterned paper, following pattern found on CD.
2. Die-cut pennants from patterned paper. Ink and curl edges; adhere to cone.
3. Fold tissue garland length-wise; adhere to cone. Adhere twine.
4. Punch borders from patterned paper strip; ink edges, affix sticker strip, and adhere.

ⓒ BOTTLE WRAP

1. Trim patterned paper strip; mat with patterned paper.
2. Adhere strip of patterned paper; zigzag-stitch seams.
3. Affix glitter flourishes and frame; adhere wrap to bottle.
4. Affix canvas border sticker to strip of patterned paper; adhere to bottle neck.
5. Tie ribbon in bow around bottle neck; wrap with twine.
6. Thread button with twine and adhere. Stamp sentiment on label sticker; tie label to bow with twine.

ⓓ INVITATION

1. Print party details on cardstock.
2. Apply chandelier rub-on
3. Trim and adhere doily die-cut; wrap with ribbon and tie in knot.

ⓔ TREAT BAG

1. Trim cardstock into 12" x 2½" strip; stamp spider web.
2. Score at 5", 6", and 11"; fold at each score and adhere 1" flap to underside of 5" stamped piece.
3. Trim strip of patterned paper; ink edges and adhere.
4. Die-cut label, ink edges, stamp frame, and apply rub-on.
5. Wrap tinsel and twine around top; attach label with ends of tinsel and adhere label to bag with foam tape.

ⓕ CUPCAKE TOPPER

1. Adhere tinsel to outer edge of felt circle.
2. Adhere ribbon behind piece, pleating as you go.
3. Adhere skewers to backs.

ⓖ FAVOR BAG

1. Trim rectangle of patterned paper. Trim doily die-cut to fit; adhere.
2. Pleat and adhere ribbon; wrap with twine. Adhere button and affix glitter pearls.
3. Trim label from patterned paper; ink edges, trim, and adhere.
4. Apply poison and fly rub-ons and affix canvas border.
5. Tie ribbon around label piece, wrap with twine, and affix badge.

ⓗ HAT TABLE SETTING

1. Make hat from patterned paper, following pattern found on CD; ink edges and roll brim into curve.
2. Adhere polka dot and bat trim.
3. Punch circle from patterned paper and apply boo rub-on; adhere tinsel.
4. Stamps bats on cardstock; emboss, trim, and adhere.
5. Adhere piece to hat.

ⓘ CENTERPIECE

1. Make cone tree from patterned paper; trim with decorative-edge scissors.
2. Punch butterflies from patterned paper; adhere.
3. Insert skewer; adhere.
4. Ink pot, insert floral foam, and insert skewer. Cover with moss and adhere to chipboard circle.
5. Trim skeleton image from patterned paper and adhere to small tag; ink edges. Adhere tinsel; affix glitter pearls.
6. Adhere patterned paper to medium tag. Ink edges, deboss words, and color with marker. Adhere trim. Stamp crow on patterned paper; trim and adhere. Affix glitter pearls.
7. Adhere patterned paper to large tag; ink edges. Deboss words; color with marker. Emboss web and spider. Stamp bats on patterned paper; trim and adhere with foam tape. Adhere ribbon to base; wrap with twine. Adhere bat trim pieces; affix glitter pearls.
8. Adhere tag gravestones to chipboard circle; adhere moss.

Designer Tip

Invitation wording can be found on included CD.

CALLING ALL GOBLINS, GHOSTS
AND FREAKS OF FRIGHT!
CREEP, FLOAT OR CRAWL
OVER TO OUR
Spooktacular Soiree
ON SATURDAY, OCTOBER 31ST
AT 6:00PM
123 HOCUS POCUS WAY

Costume Party

Designer: Kelley Eubanks

ⓐ BANNER

1. Die-cut banner flags from burlap; paint.
2. Die-cut banner flags from patterned paper panels; ink and adhere to burlap banner flags with foam tape.
3. Paint chipboard alphabet and let dry; distress. Adhere to banner flags to spell "Boo".
4. Affix stickers to banner flags.
5. Set eyelets, thread twine through banner flags, and tie bows.

ⓑ PLACE CARD

Ink all edges.

1. Make place card from patterned paper.
2. Stamp name on cardstock; trim and adhere with foam tape. Adhere chipboard bird and pumpkin.
3. Adhere rhinestone.

ⓒ TREAT BOX

Ink all edges.

1. Die-cut box from cardstock.
2. Trim patterned paper rectangles and adhere.
3. Stamp creepy candy on cardstock; punch into circle. Thread twine through punched circle, wrap around box, and tie bow.

ⓓ INVITATION

1. Make invitation from cardstock.
2. Round bottom corners and ink edges.
3. Stamp costume party, little witch, and Frankenstein. Color images with makers.
4. Tie on twine and adhere rhinestones.

ⓔ CADDY

Ink all paper edges.

1. Paint caddy.
2. Trim patterned paper and adhere.
3. Stamp spooky; emboss.
4. Trim 2 spiders from patterned paper and adhere to twine with foam tape. Tie twine on handle.
5. Adhere rhinestone.

ⓕ CUPCAKE TOPPER

Ink all edges.

1. Punch circle from cardstock; affix stickers.
2. Adhere to punched patterned paper circle with foam tape.
3. Adhere twine around dowel.
4. Adhere dowel to embellished circle.

ⓖ CHALKBOARD

Ink all paper edges.

1. Paint chalkboard frame; let dry.
2. Punch squares from patterned paper panels and adhere to chalkboard frame.
3. Trim around frame.
4. Apply decoupage.

Try This

Use the chalkboard to tally votes for best, scariest, or silliest costume.

Cute & Whimsical Halloween

Designer: Becky Olsen

ⓐ TREAT BAG

❶ Fill treat bag with candy corn.
❷ Fold and adhere patterned paper.
❸ Hole-punch patterned paper and thread ribbon through; tie bow.
❹ Attach brad to button and adhere.
❺ Apply rub-ons to die cut to spell "Spooky treats"; adhere.

ⓑ DRINK WRAP

❶ Trim patterned paper strip to 12" x 2"; accordion-fold.
❷ Tie ribbon on tag. Attach brad.
❸ Adhere tag.

ⓒ CUPCAKE WRAP

❶ Trim 2 patterned paper strips to 12" x 2"; accordion-fold.
❷ Adhere ends together.

ⓓ CUPCAKE PICK

❶ Die-cut 2 scalloped circles from patterned paper; adhere toothpick between circles.
❷ Die-cut circles from patterned paper. Adhere together.
❸ Attach brads and adhere circle to scalloped circle with foam tape.

ⓔ INVITATION

❶ Print sentiment on patterned paper; mat with patterned paper.
❷ Hole-punch die cut, thread ribbon through, and tie bow.
❸ Attach brad to button; adhere.
❹ Slide die-cut piece over invitation.

ⓕ BANNER

❶ Trim banner flags from patterned paper panels; adhere together.
❷ Adhere glitter to chipboard letters; adhere to banner flags.
❸ Adhere glitter to banner tags.
❹ Adhere rickrack to tops of banner flags.

ⓖ MENU

❶ Print sentiment on patterned paper.
❷ Trim frame from patterned paper and adhere.
❸ Attach brads.

Designer Tip

Invitation and menu wording can be found on included CD.

Try This

Have fun naming your snacks in spooky and creative ways, like Becky did on her menu!

Marinated Mozzarella Eyes
Mummy's Famous Hummus
Deep Fried Bat Legs
Graveyard Slime Gravy
Smashed Ghost Potatoes
Frog Eye Pie

spooky treats

Please join us at our Haunted Mansion for an evening of

RIP

Halloween Mask-erade

Designer: Layle Koncar

(a) INVITATION

1. Make invitation from patterned paper.
2. Adhere floss and affix spider.
3. Trim square from patterned paper; ink edges. Affix stickers to spell "Boo!". Adhere to patterned paper panel with foam tape.
4. Adhere panel to invitation with foam tape.
5. Print sentiment on patterned paper; adhere inside invitation.

(b) MENU

1. Print sentiment on patterned paper.
2. Double mat with patterned paper.
3. Apply glitter glue.

(c) PLACE CARD

1. Make place card from patterned paper.
2. Stamp name on patterned paper; ink edges and adhere.
3. Affix stickers.

(d) TALL CANDY JAR

1. Fill jar with candy.
2. Affix stickers.

(e) SHORT CANDY JAR

1. Fill jar with candy.
2. Adhere patterned paper to top of lid.
3. Trim patterned paper strips with decorative-edge scissors; adhere.
4. Affix sticker and adhere spider.

(f) PAPER CUP

1. Trim patterned paper strip and adhere around cup.
2. Affix stickers.

(g) PUMPKIN

1. Paint pumpkin; let dry.
2. Affix sticker.

(h) TREE

1. Punch circles from patterned paper. Adhere to tree.
2. Apply glitter glue to stickers. Adhere to tree.

(i) BROOM GOODY BAG

1. Cut strips into paper bag top.
2. Fill cellophane bag with candy; place in paper bag.
3. Insert stick. Tie yarn around bag.

(j) MASK

1. Trim mask from patterned paper, following pattern found on CD.
2. Apply glitter glue.
3. Affix stickers and adhere spider.
4. Adhere ribbon strips.
5. Wrap pencil with tape; adhere to mask.

Designer Tip

Menu wording can be found on included CD

Try This

Let your guests make their own masks at the party and give prizes for the scariest, most dramatic, and cutest.

A Quaint Halloween

Designer: Michelle Keeth, courtesy of Canvas Corp.

ⓐ HALLOWEEN CANVAS

Ink all edges.

❶ Paint large and small canvas; let dry.
❷ Trim patterned paper pieces; adhere to large canvas.
❸ Adhere patterned paper square to small canvas. Trim circle from patterned paper and adhere.
❹ Trim cat from cardstock, following pattern on included disk. Adhere.
❺ Adhere small canvas to large canvas.

ⓑ WITCH

See instructions on page 286.

BROOM

ⓒ
❶ Trim patterned paper in 1" strips; ink edges. Adhere around broom stick.
❷ Ink edges of patterned paper rectangle and adhere around bristles.
❸ Trim fringe from patterned paper and adhere.
❹ Adhere patterned paper strip around broom stick.

ⓓ TREE

❶ Trim patterned paper sections. Staple ribbon pieces to one section. Adhere patterned paper sections to flower pot. Place foam in flower pot.
❷ Make tree from wire; insert in flower pot. Place floral sticks and paper strips in flower pot.
❸ Adhere patterned paper and cardstock strips to cardstock. Trim into triangles, ink edges, and adhere to either side of canvas triangles; ink edges. Attach to tree with clothespins.
❹ Trim patterned paper pieces into triangles and strips; adhere to either side of canvas triangles. Trim ovals from cardstock; adhere to form hat brim. Punch flowers from patterned paper; layer and adhere. Attach to tree with clothespins.

ⓔ SPIDER BANNER

See instructions and detailed image on page 285.

ⓕ TREAT BAG

❶ Ink bag.
❷ Hole-punch bag; tie on rope.
❸ Ink edges of patterned paper pieces. Adhere to triangles; ink edges.
❹ Stamp Trick or Treat on canvas circle. Ink edges.
❺ Attach canvas pieces to rope with mini clothespins.

ⓖ INVITATION

See instructions and detailed image on page 285.

Designer Tips

- Use fabric adhesive to adhere to burlap and canvas.

- Hang your banner vertically, horizontally, or diagonally. Simply move the pieces around as desired.

Monster Madness

Designer: Chan Vuong

ⓐ INVITATION

❶ Die-cut haunted house from cardstock panels.
❷ Paper-piece together.

ⓑ PLACEMAT

❶ Die-cut label and rounded rectangle from cardstock.
❷ Adhere die cuts together.
❸ Die-cut spider and spider web from cardstock; adhere. *Note: Use foam tape to adhere spider.*
❹ Adhere wiggle eyes.

ⓒ PLACE CARD

❶ Die-cut pumpkin from cardstock panels; paper-piece together.
❷ Affix stickers to spell name.
❸ Adhere wiggle eyes.
❹ Fold cardstock and adhere behind pumpkin for stand.

ⓓ COASTER

❶ Round corners of cardstock. Adhere to coaster.
❷ Die-cut spider web from cardstock; adhere.
❸ Adhere wiggle eyes.

ⓔ NAPKIN RING

❶ Trim cardstock strip 1¾" x 6". Adhere ends to form ring.
❷ Adhere wiggle eyes.

ⓕ FAVOR BAG

❶ Die-cut monster favor bag from cardstock panels; assemble and adhere pieces.
❷ Adhere wiggle eyes.
❸ Hole-punch medium bag and tie on rope.

ⓖ CUPCAKE TOPPER

❶ Die-cut ghost from cardstock; paper-piece together.
❷ Adhere wiggle eyes.
❸ Adhere to lollipop stick.

Try This

Use one of the monster favor bags as a prize gift bag for Best Costume.

Elegant Halloween

Designer: Renae Curtz

ⓐ TREAT BAG

❶ Affix stickers to bag.
❷ Place tissue paper in bag.
❸ Trim tombstone from cardstock; pierce edges.
❹ Die-cut "RIP" from cardstock; adhere to tombstone.
❺ Trim bat from patterned paper and adhere to tombstone with foam tape.
❻ Place tombstone in bag.

ⓑ INVITATION

❶ Make invitation from cardstock.
❷ Stamp bats. Adhere patterned paper rectangles.
❸ Pleat and adhere ribbon.
❹ Stamp spooky on cardstock; trim. Adhere with foam tape. Adhere rhinestones.
❺ Trim bats from patterned paper and adhere with foam tape.

ⓒ BANNER

❶ Die-cut banner flags from cardstock; cut off scalloped edge. Trim patterned paper and adhere.
❷ Adhere ribbon behind banner flags. *Note: Pleat ribbon as you adhere.*
❸ Die-cut letters from cardstock; adhere with foam tape.
❹ Affix stickers.
❺ Trim bats from patterned paper; adhere with foam tape.
❻ Hole-punch banner flags and tie together with ribbon.

ⓓ FRAME

❶ Spray paint frame.
❷ Insert patterned paper.

ⓔ MARTINI PICK

❶ Trim patterned paper strips; adhere around skewers.
❷ Trim bats from patterned paper; adhere with foam tape.

Try This

Use the elegant frame as your serving tray.

Spooky Halloween

Designer: Joannie McBride

ⓐ BANNER

1. Trim patterned paper. Adhere behind frames.
2. Trim image from patterned paper; adhere.
3. Affix alphabet stickers to spell sentiment. Affix remaining stickers.
4. Adhere rhinestones.
5. Adhere frames to ribbon.

ⓑ FRAME

1. Trim cardstock rectangle with decorative-edge scissors; adhere to patterned paper panel.
2. Trim patterned paper rectangle and adhere to panel.
3. Adhere ribbon around panel.
4. Affix stickers to journaling label to spell "Spooky". Attach brads.
5. Adhere journaling label with foam tape.

ⓒ INVITATION

1. Stamp invitation on journaling tag. Trim patterned paper strip and adhere.
2. Affix stickers and adhere rhinestones.
3. Thread on ribbon and attach brad.

ⓓ BAG

1. Spray bag with shimmer spray; let dry.
2. Trim patterned paper strip and adhere.
3. Attach brad through ribbon and adhere.
4. Affix sticker.

ⓔ SODA BOTTLE

1. Trim cardstock rectangle with decorative-edge scissors. Adhere around soda bottle.
2. Adhere ribbon.
3. Trim patterned paper strip and adhere.
4. Affix sticker.
5. Trim prongs from brad and adhere.

ⓕ CANDY DISH

1. Trim patterned paper and adhere around candy dish.
2. Attach brad through ribbon and adhere.

ⓖ NAPKIN RING

1. Trim patterned paper to 1" x 6½". Adhere into ring.
2. Attach brad through ribbon and adhere.

Try This

Create a soundtrack for your party that includes songs like "The Monster Mash", "Witchy Woman", and "Thriller".

Wonderland Halloween

Designer: Betsy Veldman

ⓐ FOOD SIGN

1. Make card from cardstock.
2. Adhere patterned paper and stitch border.
3. Print "Eat me" on cardstock. Die-cut decorative edge from cardstock; ink.
4. Stamp web, spider, and decorative element on die cut; adhere.
5. Trim clock from patterned paper. Adhere with foam tape.
6. Adhere rhinestone.

ⓑ SIGN

1. Trim various patterned paper and adhere to sign. Trim cardstock and adhere.
2. Sand, distress, and ink edges.
3. Adhere keyhole.

ⓒ PLACE CARD

1. Trim place card from cardstock, following pattern found on CD.
2. Print name on cardstock; stamp 10-31. Distress and ink edges; adhere.
3. Tie on ribbon.
4. Trim circle from patterned paper; adhere with foam tape.

ⓓ INVITATION

1. Make invitation from cardstock, following pattern found on CD.
2. Trim circle from patterned paper. Die-cut clock from cardstock; stamp flourishes. Adhere to patterned paper circle.
3. Trim image from patterned paper; adhere with foam tape.
4. Stamp sentiment on cardstock; adhere and trim edges.
5. Attach key to keyhole with ball chain; adhere.

ⓔ PLAYING CARD FAVOR

1. Trim patterned paper strips; adhere around playing card box.
2. Stamp rectangle frame, hearts, and 5s on cardstock. Round corners and adhere.
3. Thread key on twine; tie around box.
4. Trim image from patterned paper; adhere with foam tape.

ⓕ BOTTLE

1. Trim strip from patterned paper; adhere around bottle. Adhere keyhole.
2. Print "Drink me" on cardstock; trim into tag and ink edges. Stamp flourish frame.
3. Hole-punch tag, thread on twine, and tie on bottle.

Try This

- Have your guests dress as characters from "Alice in Wonderland".

- Play "Pin the Smile on the Cheshire Cat".

At Last! We thought you'd never arrive.

Drink Me

Drink Me

Hallowe'en in Wonderland
Curiouser and curiouser

Liquid Silmerine

YOU'RE INVITED TO tea

Eat Me

Alice

Hatter

Happy Halloween

Designer: Laura O'Donnell

ⓐ CUPCAKE TOPPER

❶ Punch circles from cardstock; adhere together.

❷ Punch circle from patterned paper; trim and adhere to one topper.

❸ Affix stickers. Adhere circles to toothpicks.

❹ Adhere cardstock circles behind toppers.

ⓑ CARD

❶ Make card from cardstock.

❷ Trim patterned paper rectangle, distress edges, and adhere.

❸ Stamp mummy on cardstock. Trim banner flags from image. Adhere mummy.

❹ Color banner flags with marker and adhere with foam tape.

ⓒ BANNER

❶ Trim banner flags from cardstock.

❷ Trim triangles from patterned paper. Distress edges and adhere to banner flags.

❸ Trim letters from cardstock, following pattern found on CD.

❹ Affix stickers. Hole-punch banner flags; tie together with twine.

ⓓ PHOTO FRAME

❶ Distress cardstock edges and adhere to cardboard.

❷ Adhere photo.

❸ Stamp happy Halloween on cardstock. Trim, distress edges, and adhere.

❹ Affix sticker.

ⓔ GOODIE BAG

❶ Trim patterned paper rectangle. Distress edges and adhere to bag.

❷ Stamp sentiment on cardstock; trim. Distress edges. Draw border with pen. Apply glitter glue.

❸ Adhere panel to bag. Affix stickers.

Try This

This photo frame makes a fun and easy party craft for guests to take home as a keepsake from the night.

Thanksgiving Kids' Table

Designer: Beth Opel

ⓐ PLACE CARD

1. Make place cards from patterned paper.
2. Adhere cardstock.
3. Affix letters to spell names.
4. Punch leaves from cardstock; adhere with foam tape.

ⓑ MENU

1. Trim cardstock; round corners.
2. Print menu on cardstock; trim, round corners, and adhere.
3. Adhere patterned paper strip.
4. Affix stickers to spell "Menu".
5. Punch leaf from cardstock; adhere with foam tape.

ⓒ NAPKIN RING

1. Punch circle from cardstock; adhere to flowers. Trim petals.
2. Make turkey body from cardstock, following pattern found on included CD. Adhere with foam tape.
3. Adhere wiggle eyes. Cut beak from cardstock; adhere with foam tape.
4. Cut wattle from felt; adhere.
5. Adhere turkey to ribbon.

ⓓ TURKEY

1. Repeat steps 1-4 from Napkin Ring.
2. Trim cardstock strip; fold and cut notches. Sit turkey in stand.

ⓔ THANKFUL JAR

1. Punch tag from cardstock.
2. Print sentiment on cardstock; trim and adhere.
3. Adhere patterned paper strip.
4. Tie ribbon around jar.
5. Tie tag to ribbon.

Designer Tip

Provide pencils or crayons and strips of paper for children to write what they are thankful for. Have them place the strips in the Thankful Jar.

Try This

Provide supplies for children to make their own turkeys and place cards.

b

MENU

Turkey

Mashed Potatoes

Corn

Milk

Pumpkin Pie

e

I Thank God For...

c

DAVID

LEXIE

JONNY

a

d

Classy Thanksgiving

Designer: Windy Robinson

ⓐ BANNER

1. Make rosettes from patterned paper and cardstock.
2. Punch scalloped circles from cardstock; trim and adhere.
3. Affix stickers to spell "Welcome."
4. Punch holes and thread rosettes together with twine.

ⓑ BOX

1. Adhere patterned paper strips to box.
2. Tie on ribbon.
3. Print "Our blessings" on cardstock; trim into tag.
4. Punch hole and tie on tag with twine.

ⓒ THANKFUL CARD

1. Make card from cardstock.
2. Trim and adhere patterned paper strip; punch and adhere patterned paper strip.
3. Stamp thankful.

ⓓ PLACE CARD

1. Make card from cardstock.
2. Trim and fold cardstock into envelope; adhere.
3. Print name on cardstock; trim into banner, mat with patterned paper, trim, and adhere.
4. Insert Thankful Card.

ⓔ CANDLE HOLDER

1. Cut large circle from cardstock.
2. Trace bottom of candle in middle of circle.
3. Make rosette from patterned paper and adhere, leaving center circle open for candle.
4. Place candle.

ⓕ HANGING DECORATIONS

1. Make rosettes from patterned paper and cardstock.
2. Adhere smallest rosette to largest rosette.
3. Adhere ribbon bows.
4. Punch holes and thread with twine.

ⓖ MENU

1. Double-mat patterned paper frame with patterned paper and cardstock.
2. Print "Menu" on cardstock; mat with cardstock and adhere.
3. Stamp leaf.

ⓗ FAVOR BAG

1. Make bag from patterned paper, following pattern found on CD.
2. Trim and adhere patterned paper strip; punch and adhere patterned paper strip.
3. Cinch top; punch hole and thread with twine.

ⓘ NAPKIN RING

1. Trim patterned paper strip; mat with patterned paper and adhere ends.

Try This

After guests have written blessings from the past year on their thankful cards, place them in the box. Store them away as a family keepsake for years to come.

A Homey Thanksgiving

Designer: Cristina Kowalczyk

ⓐ PLACEMAT

1. Cut canvas pieces 13" square, 13" x 18", and 2" x 13".
2. Cut burlap piece 4" x 13".
3. Stitch burlap to edge of square canvas piece.
4. Stitch smallest canvas piece to edge of burlap.
5. Stitch largest canvas piece to back; turn right side out.
6. Iron and top-stitch edges.
7. Die-cut leaves and adhere.

ⓑ NAPKIN RING and CANDLE WRAP

1. Stamp give thanks on cardstock strip; mat with burlap. Adhere ends.
2. Die-cut leaves and adhere.
3. Tie on twine.

ⓒ GARLAND

1. Die-cut leaves.
2. Stitch together.

ⓓ PLACE CARD

1. Make card from cardstock.
2. Repeat steps 2-3 from Napkin Ring and Candle Wrap.
3. Write name with pen.

ⓔ WALL HANGING

1. Trim cardstock.
2. Attach eyelets and thread with twine; mat with burlap.
3. Die-cut leaves; adhere in circle.
4. Stamp give thanks on leaf; adhere with foam tape.

Designer Tip

For more detail, stamp leaves on cardstock before die-cutting.

Try This

Stick to natural elements for additional décor. Gather twigs and make a coordinating vase wrap.

Harvest Celebration

Designer: Chan Vuong

ⓐ INVITATION

❶ Stamp invitation details and dotted lines on cardstock; trim and round corners.

❷ Punch border from patterned paper and adhere; round corners.

❸ Die-cut fox from cardstock; adhere with foam tape.

ⓑ PLACEMAT

❶ Die-cut frame from patterned paper; die-cut rectangle from patterned paper and adhere.

❷ Die-cut leaves from cardstock and adhere.

ⓒ PLACE CARD

❶ Make card from cardstock and round corners.

❷ Repeat step 2 from Invitation.

❸ Die-cut acorn from cardstock; adhere with foam tape.

❹ Affix stickers to spell name.

ⓓ NAPKIN RING

❶ Trim patterned paper strip; adhere ends.

❷ Die-cut leaf from cardstock and adhere.

ⓔ FAVOR BAG

❶ Punch top edge of bag.

❷ Trim patterned paper; punch edge and round corners. Adhere.

❸ Die-cut squirrel and leaves from cardstock; adhere with foam tape.

ⓕ CUPCAKE TOPPER

❶ Die-cut tree from cardstock; adhere.

❷ Adhere to lollipop stick.

Designer Tip

Bend up the edges of leaves on the placemat and napkin ring for dimension.

Try This

Go for a walk and collect beautiful leaves before dinner; arrange them in a bowl as a centerpiece.

for ....
on ....
at ....
by ....
rsvp ....

Dad

Thanksgiving Dinner

Designer: Renae Curtz

ⓐ MENU

1. Print text on cardstock; mat with cardstock.
2. Stamp border on cardstock; trim and adhere.
3. Stamp leaf on cardstock; fussy-cut and adhere with foam tape.

ⓑ NAPKIN RING

1. Trim cardstock strip; adhere and stitch edge.
2. Stamp leaves on cardstock; fussy-cut and adhere with foam tape.
3. Thread button with floss and adhere.

ⓒ BOX

1. Trim and adhere cardstock to box.
2. Wrap twine around box.
3. Stamp with gratitude on cardstock; trim and adhere with foam tape.
4. Stamp leaf on cardstock; fussy-cut and adhere.
5. Tie on twine.

ⓓ PINECONE PLACE TAG

1. Print name on cardstock.
2. Trim into tag.
3. Stamp leaf.
4. Punch hole, thread with twine, and attach to pinecone.

ⓔ PLACEMAT

1. Stamp leaves on cardstock.
2. Trim and adhere cardstock strip.
3. Punch and adhere cardstock strip. Stitch.

ⓕ CANDLE CENTERPIECE

1. Place candle in votive candle holder inside vase.
2. Add potpourri.
3. Wrap twine around vase.
4. Stamp leaves on cardstock; fussy-cut and adhere with foam tape.
5. Tie on twine.

Try This

Bring nature inside by decorating with things like pinecones, gourds, and pumpkins.

Tapenade

Saddle-up Sweet Potatoes

Prosciutto and Cauliflower

Candied Carrots

Garlic Mashed Potatoes

Roasted Turkey

Pumpkin Pie

With Gratitude

Mom

A Cocoa Christmas

Designer: Stephanie Halinski

ⓐ TIN

1. Trim and adhere patterned paper.
2. Adhere ribbon border.
3. Affix border sticker to lip of lid.
4. Adhere joy label with foam tape; adhere rhinestones.
5. Tie on ribbon.

ⓑ INVITATION

1. Print text on cardstock. Trim and mat on cardstock.
2. Trim and adhere patterned paper block.
3. Trim snowflake from patterned paper; adhere with foam tape. Adhere ribbon.
4. Tie on twine.

ⓒ MENU CARD

1. Make card from cardstock.
2. Print text on cardstock; affix tab sticker. Adhere.
3. Attach brad to peppermint. Adhere peppermint and snowflake stickers with foam tape. Affix sentiment sticker.
4. Adhere pearls. Tie on twine.

ⓓ TREAT BAG

1. Trim patterned paper; mat with cardstock.
2. Affix sentiment sticker.
3. Thread button with twine; adhere.
4. Tie twine around bag; clip on tag with clothespin.

ⓔ TREAT JAR

1. Write "Yum!" on label with marker; affix label. Adhere rhinestone.
2. Tie on twine.

ⓕ MUG SLEEVE

1. Trim cardboard to almost fit around mug.
2. Punch holes at ends; thread ribbon through and tie.
3. Adhere cocoa label with foam tape; adhere pearl.

Designer Tips

- When making multiple invitations, keep the design simple, and use elements like buttons and twine so that you can easily reproduce it.

- If your guest list is large, just tie ribbons around the cups and mugs for a simple, festive solution.

- Invitation and menu card templates can be found on included CD.

Try This

Use gingerbread, peppermint, and vanilla flavors in your cocoa creations for fragrant and delicious beverages.

f

Mnmm

c

Wish List

Choose your cocoa...

- Milk Chocolate
- Dark Chocolate
- Chocolate Peppermint

...then select a sweet treat

- Sugar Cookies
- Red-Velvet Cupcake
- Gingerbread Loaf

milk & cookies

b

Join us...

for warm cocoa,
yummy sweets

and

merry moments

Saturday, December 22
8 o'clock
at Stephanie's
RSVP by December 15

JOY

d

Just for you

a

e

yum!

Christmas in the Old Days

Designer: Nina Brackett

ⓐ BANNER

1. Die-cut decorative-edged pennants from cardstock. Die-cut pennants from patterned paper; ink edges and adhere.
2. Adhere doilies.
3. Make 3" rosette; adhere. *Note: See sidebar.*
4. Trim square from cardstock; round corners, ink edges, and adhere with foam tape.
5. Affix alphabet stickers to spell "Joy" and "Noel". Affix remaining stickers. *Note: Use foam tape on some.*
6. Adhere rhinestones and buttons.
7. Punch holes and tie pennants together with twill.

ⓑ CUPCAKE TOPPER

1. Make 2½" rosette; adhere to lollipop stick .
2. Punch circles from cardstock; ink edges and mat with cardstock circle. Adhere to punched scalloped circle and adhere to rosette.
3. Affix sticker.
4. Thread button with twine and adhere. Tie on trim.

ⓒ INVITATION

1. Trim cardstock; ink edges.
2. Trim patterned paper with decorative-edge scissors. Adhere and stitch edges.
3. Print text on cardstock; ink and adhere.
4. Cut patterned paper corners, using decorative-edge scissors on one edge; ink and adhere.
5. Adhere buttons and twill bow.

ⓓ HYMN BOOKLET

1. Print hymns on cardstock.
2. Trim cardstock cover and back.
3. Trim patterned paper with decorative-edge scissors; stitch edges and adhere.
4. Trim patterned paper strip; adhere. Adhere doily.
5. Stamp music label on cardstock; die-cut label, ink edges, and adhere.
6. Print title; die-cut and emboss circle, ink, and adhere with foam tape.
7. Thread buttons with twine and adhere.
8. Punch holes in covers and pages; thread with twill and tie bow.

ⓔ THANK YOU CARD

1. Make card from cardstock.
2. Trim and adhere patterned paper strips.
3. Trim and adhere doily.
4. Tie on twill.
5. Stamp label on cardstock; die-cut label, ink edges, and adhere with foam tape.
6. Stamp thank you on cardstock; die-cut circle, ink edges, and adhere with foam tape.
7. Thread buttons with twine and adhere.

ⓕ ORNAMENT

1. Make 4" rosette.
2. Pleat and adhere trim.
3. Stamp globe on cardstock; mat with die cut patterned paper flower. Adhere.
4. Stamp joy on cardstock; die-cut oval, ink edges, and adhere.
5. Adhere twill bow. Punch hole and thread twill through for hanger.
6. Thread button with twine and adhere.

ⓖ TREAT TUBE

1. Trim tube and fill with treats.
2. Wrap patterned paper around tube and adhere.
3. Tie twill bows at each end.
4. Adhere doily.
5. Trim postcard from patterned paper; distress edges, mat with cardstock, and adhere.
6. Thread buttons with twine and adhere.

How to Create a Rosette

1. Cut 2 strips of 12" paper. Note: The wider the strip, the larger the rosette. Finished rosette will be approximately twice the diameter of the strip width.
2. Score strips at ½" intervals.
3. Accordion fold and adhere end to end.
4. Punch two circles. Form rosette and adhere circles to front and back.

Designer Tip

Invitation template and hymns can be found on included CD.

Try This

Ask guests to bring a handmade or vintage ornament to exchange.

Sweet and Snowy Christmas

Designer: Tanis Giesbrecht

ⓐ BOTTLE WRAP

1. Trim patterned paper and punch edge.
2. Trim and adhere patterned paper; punch, trim, and adhere cardstock border.
3. Trim pennants from patterned paper. Affix stickers to cardstock to spell "Merry"; trim and adhere. Punch circle from cardstock; attach with staples. Punch holes in pennants and thread with twine; adhere. Punch holes in base and thread with twine; tie.
4. Fussy-cut snowflake from patterned paper; adhere. Adhere button.
5. Wrap around bottle and adhere.

ⓑ PLACE CARD

1. Make card from cardstock; round bottom corners.
2. Trim patterned paper strips; round corners of one. Adhere.
3. Punch border from cardstock; adhere and stitch.
4. Affix stickers to spell name.
5. Affix snowman and Santa.

ⓒ TREAT BOX

1. Make box, following pattern found on CD.
2. Trim and adhere cardstock.
3. Trim patterned paper and punch corners; adhere.
4. Punch border from patterned paper; adhere. Affix stickers to spell "Thanks."
5. Affix heart and snowflake stickers. Adhere pearl.
6. Tie on twine.

ⓓ CUPCAKE TOPPER

1. Punch scalloped circle from patterned paper.
2. Punch circle from cardstock; adhere.
3. Affix snowman and snowflake stickers.
4. Trim patterned paper into banner; affix stickers to spell "Mmm" and "Yum." Attach with staples.
5. Adhere twine for scarf.
6. Thread button with twine and adhere.
7. Trim skewer and adhere between circles.

ⓔ NAPKIN RING

1. Trim muslin; fold and adhere into 1¼" x 6" strip.
2. Trim patterned paper; stitch to muslin.
3. Roll into ring and adhere.
4. Fussy-cut snowflake from patterned paper; mat with cardstock, trim, and adhere.
5. Thread button with twine and adhere.

Designer Tip

Clip the cupcake topper sides together with clothespins or paperclips as they dry.

Try This

Thrill the children at your party by making a large replica of the snowman and playing "Pin the Buttons on the Snowman."

Elegant Christmas

Designer: Windy Robinson

ⓐ PLACE CARD

❶ Make card from cardstock.
❷ Trim patterned paper; ink edges and adhere.
❸ Print name on cardstock; trim into banner and adhere.

ⓑ INVITATION

❶ Repeat steps 1-2 from Place Card.
❷ Trim patterned paper strip; ink edges and adhere. Zigzag-stitch edge.
❸ Trim and adhere cardstock strip.
❹ Print "An invitation" on cardstock; trim into banner and adhere.
❺ Adhere ribbon bow; tie on stars with twine.

ⓒ CHAIN

❶ Make interlocking chain with strips of patterned paper.
❷ Tie on stars with twine.

ⓓ MENU

❶ Make tri-fold card from patterned paper; ink edges. Print menu on cardstock and slip inside.
❷ Print "Menu" on cardstock; trim into banner and adhere to cardstock strip. Mat with cardstock; wrap around card and adhere ends.
❸ Tie on ribbon; tie on stars with twine.

ⓔ POPPERS

❶ Roll strip of patterned paper; adhere.
❷ Insert rolls inside pretzel bags; fill with treats and trim off excess bag. Thread twine through stars and tie ends.
❸ Print "Merry Christmas" on cardstock; trim into banners and adhere with foam tape.

ⓕ NAPKIN RING

❶ Mat patterned paper strip with cardstock; zigzag-stitch edges. Adhere ends.
❷ Tie on ribbon; tie on stars with twine.

ⓖ TREES

❶ Cut four equal triangles from patterned paper; ink edges and fold each in half vertically. Adhere.
❷ Tie on ribbon; tie on stars with twine.

Designer Tip

Make your party ensemble less complicated by sticking to two patterned papers and two colors of cardstock.

An Invitation

Menu

Merry Christmas

Merry Christmas

Rebecca

A Very Deer Christmas

Designer: Betsy Veldman

ⓐ TRAY

1. Trim patterned paper panels.
2. Adhere to tray with decoupage.

ⓑ BOTTLE WRAP and TAG

1. Trim patterned paper and wrap around bottle.
2. Affix border strip.
3. Die-cut label from patterned paper; ink edges and adhere.
4. Die-cut circle from cardstock; stamp deer and cheers. Ink edges and adhere. Adhere pearls.
5. Die-cut deer from cardstock; adhere greenery and pearls.
6. Punch hole and thread ball chain through; attach to bottle neck

ⓒ INVITATION

Ink all edges.

1. Trim patterned paper block; round corners.
2. Trim patterned paper; stitch patterned paper strip to top edge. Stitch to base on three sides to form pocket.
3. Die-cut circle from patterned paper; adhere.
4. Stamp deer on cardstock; punch into circle and mat with circle-punched cardstock. Adhere with foam tape.
5. Make tag from cardstock. Print or write party information.
6. Stamp you're invited.
7. Punch hole; attach eyelet and tie on ribbon.
8. Insert tag into pocket.

ⓓ COASTER

Ink all edges.

1. Die-cut circles from patterned paper.
2. Die-cut deer from smaller circles and mat with larger circle.
3. With deer in cut, stitch edges. *Note: Stitch down legs but not antlers.*
4. Print name on cardstock; trim into tag.
5. Punch hole and tie on twine.

ⓔ NAPKIN RING

1. Trim patterned paper strip. Adhere ends.
2. Die-cut flower from patterned paper; ink edges, assemble, and adhere.
3. Adhere greenery.
4. Die-cut deer from cardstock; adhere.

ⓕ GARLAND

1. Die-cut deer from cardstock.
2. Adhere antlers and feet.
3. Adhere greenery and pearls.

Try This

Encourage guests to wear cozy sweaters and flannel shirts to go with the cabin vibe.

Tree Trimming

Designer: Julia Stainton

ⓐ INVITATION

1. Make card from cardstock.
2. Trim and adhere patterned paper block and strip.
3. Cut patterned paper strip with decorative-edge scissors; adhere.
4. Print sentiment on cardstock; trim and attach with staples.
5. Affix stickers; adhere rhinestones. Tie on twine; attach pin.

ⓑ GIFT BAG

1. Trim and adhere patterned paper to bag.
2. Affix border sticker.
3. Die-cut ornament from cardstock; ink edges. Apply rub-on; adhere button and rhinestone. Adhere to bag; tie on twine.

ⓒ MENU

1. Trim chipboard; adhere patterned paper.
2. Print text on vellum; attach to clip and adhere.
3. Tie on twine.
4. Attach brad to sticker; affix stickers.
5. Adhere rhinestone.

ⓓ ORNAMENT

1. Apply rub-on to ornament.
2. Adhere rhinestone.

ⓔ TREES

1. Cut strips of patterned paper with decorative-edge scissors; adhere in spirals to cover foam cones.
2. Attach canvas stars with pins.
3. Tie on twine.

Designer Tip

Tacky dry adhesive strips work perfectly for adhering fringe strips to trees.

Try This

Set up tables with ornament crafts for guests to create and take home with them in the gift bags.

©

Menu

Swedish Snowball Meatballs
Holiday Pinwheel Appetizers
Festive Cheeseball
Red & Green Bruschetta
Popcorn Balls
Christmas Tree Sugar Cookies
Gingerbread Snowflake Cookies
Candy Cane Bark
Cranberry Punch
Hot Mulled Cider

ⓔ

Deck the Halls, Deck the Halls, Deck the Halls

ⓐ

ⓑ

ⓓ

Let Heaven and Nature Sing

Designer: Sarah Jay

ⓐ WREATH

1. Cut burlap into strips; pull fibers on edges to distress.
2. Wrap burlap around foam wreath; attach with pins.
3. Spray cardstock with shimmer spray; hand cut leaves. Score and attach with pins.
4. Stamp Circle Lace on vellum; heat set. Hand cut leaves; attach with pins. Die-cut flowers; adhere. Punch circle from sprayed cardstock; adhere.
5. Stamp cardstock with Music Notes. Trim, fold, cut into banner, and attach with pins.
6. Spray alphabet stickers with shimmer spray; heat set and affix to spell "Peace".
7. Attach branches with pins. Tie on lace.

ⓑ GIFT BAG

1. Stamp Circle Lace on bag; heat set.
2. Tie on burlap strip.
3. Spray cardstock with shimmer spray; hand cut and score leaves. Punch heart.
4. Die-cut heart and tag from cardstock; stamp tag with Music Notes. Stamp for you on heart.
5. Tie on leaves, hearts, and tag with floss; adhere with foam tape.

ⓒ MENU and INVITATION

1. Print text on vellum; stamp Circle Lace and heat set.
2. Mat with cardstock.
3. Tie on burlap strip.
4. Die-cut tag from cardstock; stamp with Music Notes. Tie on with floss.

ⓓ THANK YOU CARD

1. Make card from cardstock.
2. Print text on vellum; stamp Circle Lace and heat set.

ⓔ PLACE CARD

1. Make card from cardstock.
2. Stamp Circle Lace on vellum; heat set, trim, and adhere.
3. Spray cardstock with shimmer spray; hand cut leaves. Score and tie on twine.
4. Spray alphabet stickers with shimmer spray; heat set and affix to spell name.

ⓕ ORNAMENT

1. Stamp Circle Lace on vellum; heat set, trim into circle, and insert into ornament. *Note: See Sidebar.*
2. Tie on burlap strip.
3. Repeat step 3 from Place Card.

Designer Tips

- Stamp on reverse side of vellum for a softer look. Heat set stamped vellum before handling to discourage smudging.

- With maroon, navy, or plum cardstock and a coordinating shimmer spray, this ensemble could go from rustic to elegant.

- Invitation and menu templates can be found on included CD.

Try This

Serve comfort food and light a cozy fire for a warm setting before you head out on your sleigh ride.

a

f

b

c

c

Menu
Curried Butternut Squash Soup
with crème fraîche

Warm Spinach Salad
with apples, pecans, and goat cheese
in apple vinaigrette

Spice Rubbed Roast Chicken
and cranberry compote
with roasted winter vegetables

Cheese and Fruit Plate

Apple Tart
with spiced honey glaze
and cranberry cardamom ice cream

Served with
Cadillac Mountain Stout
Bar Harbor Brewing Company
2008 Crane Lake Petite Sirah (CA)

Please join us for
a winter's sleigh ride,
joyous carols, and a

Holiday Dinner
Saturday, December 17th at 6pm

The Johnson Homestead
4124 Cedar Lane, Bedford

please remember to bring
weather-appropriate outerwear
RSVP to Amy by December 12th

Thank You

Susan

d

e

Festive Christmas

Designer: Renae Curtz

ⓐ CARD
1. Make card from cardstock.
2. Affix merry Christmas and border stickers; stitch center strip.
3. Thread button with twine and adhere.

ⓑ BOX
1. Die-cut matchbox from cardstock; assemble.
2. Punch label from cardstock; punch holes, thread with twill, and adhere.
3. Punch circle from patterned paper; adhere with foam tape.
4. Adhere rhinestone.

ⓒ ORNAMENT
1. Die-cut circle from cardstock.
2. Punch circle from patterned paper; adhere with foam tape.
3. Punch hole and thread with twine.
4. Adhere rhinestone.

ⓓ JAR
1. Punch holes in label; thread with twill, wrap around jar, and adhere.
2. Affix stickers to spell "Joy".

ⓔ CANVAS
1. Trim and adhere patterned paper to canvas.
2. Affix border stickers.
3. Thread button with twine and adhere.
4. Die-cut letters from cardstock; adhere to spell "Noel". *Note: Adhere letters with foam tape.*

Try This

Hide a wish list inside each matchbox and use them to exchange names for a family or between colleagues.

noel

Merry Christmas~

joy

noel

Shabby Chic Christmas

Designer: Carolyn Peeler, courtesy of Melissa Frances

ⓐ INVITATION

Ink all edges.

1. Trim patterned paper strip; adhere to note card.
2. Cut cardstock strip with decorative-edge scissors and adhere; trim and adhere patterned paper.
3. Spray seam binding with shimmer spray; tie around card.
4. Trim and adhere ticket.
5. Apply rub-on to cardstock; trim into banner and adhere.
6. Die-cut rose from cardstock; roll and adhere.
7. Adhere button and rhinestone.

ⓑ ORNAMENTS

1. Trim chipboard to fit inside frames; cover backs with patterned paper.
2. Adhere ribbon loops. Affix stickers to chipboard fronts.
3. Adhere chipboard pieces to frames.

ⓒ PLACE CARD

1. Trim and adhere patterned paper strip to envelope. Border-punch patterned paper strip and adhere.
2. Write name on circle tags with pen; adhere with foam tape.
3. Spray seam binding with shimmer spray; thread though tag and tie.
4. Thread button with floss and adhere.

ⓓ BANNER

1. Cut pennants from chipboard; adhere patterned paper.
2. Cut squares from chipboard; adhere patterned paper and trim. Stitch edges and adhere.
3. Ink scalloped chipboard strips; apply glitter glue. Trim and adhere; adhere pearls.
4. Trim patterned paper strip; score, fold, and adhere into rosette; adhere.
5. Adhere chipboard letters to spell "Joy".
6. Attach rhinestone drops with thread; adhere buttons and pearls.
7. Punch holes in banner shapes and thread ribbon through.

Designer Tip

Use denim weight needle to stitch through chipboard.

Try This

Use the tags inside the place card envelopes to write a personal note to each of your guests.

Homey Holiday Party

Designer: Latisha Yoast

ⓐ TALL TREAT BAG

1. Trim patterned paper; adhere to bag.
2. Wrap ribbon around bag; tie with twine.
3. Stamp label and sentiment on patterned paper; die-cut and emboss. Adhere with foam tape.

ⓑ TIN

1. Adhere patterned paper strip to tin.
2. Tie on ribbon.
3. Repeat step 3 from Tall Treat Bag.

ⓒ SMALL TREAT BAG

1. Stamp sentiment on bag.
2. Tie on trim.
3. Thread button with twine and tie to trim.

ⓓ WHITE TREAT BAG

1. Stamp sentiment on cardstock; mat on patterned paper and punch edge.
2. Adhere trim. Adhere to bag.
3. Stamp ornament on cardstock; die-cut and emboss.
4. Adhere pearl and adhere ornament with foam tape.

ⓔ CARD

1. Make card from cardstock.
2. Stamp ornament and sentiment.
3. Tie on ribbon.
4. Adhere pearls.

ⓕ GIFT BAG

1. Die-cut and emboss rectangle from patterned paper; adhere to bag.
2. Stamp happy holidays on cardstock; trim and adhere.
3. Stamp ornament on cardstock; die-cut and emboss. Adhere with foam tape.
4. Adhere pearls.

ⓖ ACCORDION TAG HOLDER

1. Make holder from cardstock.
2. Trim and adhere patterned paper on three sides on each panel; adhere trim.
3. Stamp sentiments and mittens on cardstock.
4. Die-cut and emboss tags; punch hole and thread ribbon through. Tie on twine.
5. Insert tags in folder pockets.

Designer Tip

Keep things simple by sticking to one main color and offsetting it with neutrals.

Try This

Invite your friends over for a cookie exchange or gift wrap party. Supply lots of plain bags for guests to decorate.

Classy Christmas

Designer: Michelle Rasmussen, courtesy of Lifestyle Crafts

ⓐ INVITATION with ENVELOPE

❶ Create custom text with your specific party details at *www.LifestyleCrafts.com*.

❷ Deboss and ink damask and celebrate Christmas on paper.

❸ Die-cut belly band from paper; deboss and ink text and border; wrap around card and adhere ends.

❹ Die-cut envelope liner from vellum; die-cut branch from cardstock and adhere. Adhere inside envelope.

ⓑ FRAME

❶ Deboss and ink tree on specialty paper.

❷ Insert in frame.

ⓒ MILK JAR

❶ Die-cut branch from cardstock. Punch circles from ribbon and adhere. Adhere to jar.

❷ Print sentiment on specialty paper.

❸ Deboss; adhere ends. Adhere to jar.

RECIPE CARD

ⓓ ❶ Deboss and ink damask on specialty paper.

❷ Print recipe on specialty paper.

❸ Deboss and ink branch and text on recipe. Trim and mat on damask paper.

ⓔ OVAL JAR LABEL

❶ Die-cut oval from paper.

❷ Deboss and ink damask; adhere.

Try This

Invite your guests to bring gifts to donate to a favorite charity.

b

a

Celebrate Christmas

December 10, 2012
6 p.m. - 9 p.m.
Rasmussen Home

c

Merry Christmas
and to all a good night

e

chocolate chip cookies

d

Hanukkah Celebration

Designer: Teri Anderson

ⓐ MENORAH

1. Adhere two tea light holders bottom to bottom.
2. Trim strip of cardstock; mat with cardstock and adhere.
3. Stamp star on cardstock; cut out and adhere.
4. Adhere rhinestone.
5. Create menorah with stacked candle in center and four tea light holders on each side. Add tea lights.

ⓑ INVITATION

1. Using pattern on included CD, cut dreidel shape from cardstock.
2. Print text on vellum; adhere.
3. Trim and adhere cardstock strips; adhere rhinestones.

ⓒ PLACEMAT

1. Trim and adhere cardstock strips to cardstock.
2. Stamp stars on cardstock; cut out and adhere.
3. Adhere rhinestone.

ⓓ PLACE CARD

1. Using pattern on included CD, cut dreidel shape from cardstock.
2. Print name on cardstock; mat with cardstock and adhere.
3. Adhere rhinestone.

ⓔ NAPKIN RING

1. Trim strip of cardstock; adhere cardstock strip. Adhere ends.
2. Tie on ribbon.
3. Repeat steps 3-4 from Menorah.

ⓕ FAVOR

1. Cut envelope, using pattern found on included CD.
2. Trim and adhere transparency; insert coins.
3. Repeat steps 3-4 from Menorah.
4. Print sentiment on cardstock; trim and adhere cardstock strip. Wrap around envelope and adhere ends.

ⓖ MENU

1. Print text on cardstock; mat with cardstock.
2. Trim and adhere cardstock strips.
3. Adhere ribbon.
4. Repeat steps 3-4 from Menorah.

ⓗ DRINK CHARM

1. Punch circles from cardstock and adhere together.
2. Cut dreidel shape from cardstock.
3. Adhere cardstock strip and rhinestone.
4. Punch hole and attach binder ring.

Designer Tip

Menu template can be found on included CD.

Try This

Sing Hanukkah songs and recite prayers or Psalms.

g

Menu

Potato Latkes with Smoked Salmon
Potato Latkes with 5-spice Apple Sauce

Fresh Green Beans with Garlic and Thyme
Filet of Beef Tenderloins

Jam-filled Donuts
Tuiles

Wine
Water

Thanks for sharing the light with us.

f

a

b

Let's share in the light.

Join us for a night to celebrate Hanukkah.

We will feast on a delicious meal.
We will light the Menorah.
And we will spin the dreidel.

The party begins at 7 p.m. Friday.
Sylvia and Jon's house

h

d

Sylvia

e

c

Kwanzaa Gathering

Designer: Teri Anderson

ⓐ UNITY CUP

❶ Trim and adhere cardstock strips to glass.
❷ Print text on cardstock; trim and adhere.
❸ Tie on twine.

ⓑ INVITATION and BOOKMARK

❶ Print text on cardstock; round corners, trim, and adhere to cardstock.
❷ Using pattern on included CD, cut candles and flames from cardstock; adhere.
❸ Tie on twine.

ⓒ FRAME

❶ Trim cardstock panel to fit frame.
❷ Trim and adhere cardstock strips.
❸ Print text on cardstock; adhere.
❹ Repeat steps 2-3 from Invitation and Bookmark.
❺ Remove glass from frame and insert panel.

ⓓ NAPKIN RING

❶ Trim strip of cardstock; adhere cardstock strips. Adhere ends.
❷ Tie on twine.

ⓔ PLACE CARD

❶ Make card from cardstock.
❷ Print name on cardstock; trim, round corners, and adhere.
❸ Using pattern on included CD, cut candles and flame from cardstock; adhere.
❹ Tie on twine.

ⓕ KINARA BASE and CANDLES

❶ Cut base from cardstock, following pattern found on included CD.
❷ Trim and adhere cardstock strips to base and around tea lights.
❸ Arrange tea lights on base.

Designer Tips

• Insert a rectangular piece of foam inside the kinara base for stability.

• Sentiments for these projects can be found on included CD.

Try This

Have guests share stories of those who have been inspirational to them.

(a)

(b) Let's celebrate Kwanzaa together!

You are invited to Mary's house on Saturday.
We'll drink from the Unity cup.
We'll share in a feast.
And we'll talk bout the principles of Kwanzaa.

The festivities begin at 5 p.m.
555-1212
Regrets only.

(c) Celebrate Kwanzaa today and tomorrow

(d)

(e) Robert

(b) Kuumba is creativity.
To do always as much as we can, in a way that we can do,
in order to leave our community more beautiful than when we inherited it.

(f)

BADGE FAVOR from BIRTHDAY
CAMP OUT Ensemble *p. 48.*

Designer: *Sarah Jay*

PLACE CARD & GIFT BOX from ROMANTIC
WEDDING SHOWER Ensemble *p. 76.*

Designer: *Ashley Cannon Newell*

CINNAMON BUN FAVOR
from BUN IN THE OVEN BABY
SHOWER Ensemble p. 94

Designer: Julie Campbell

Bingo Box from CHILDREN'S GAME
NIGHT Birthday Ensemble p. 134.

Designer: Anabelle O'Malley

INVITATION from SUMMER
PICNIC Ensemble p. 208.

Designer: Melissa Phillips

GUIDE BOOK from WINE TASTING
PARTY Ensemble p. 142.

Designer: Michelle Keeth, courtesy
of Canvas Corp.

BOW DECORATION
From **A FESTIVE 4TH OF JULY** Ensemble *p. 222*

Designer: *Courtesy of Canvas Corp.*

1. Make bow from mesh.
2. Wrap floral wires with chenille.
3. Die-cut stars from patterned paper and ink edges. Mat with burlap stars.
4. Cut stars from cardstock and patterned paper, using canvas star as template; ink edges. Mat with canvas stars and adhere. Adhere stars to chenille stems.
5. Tie on ribbons.
6. Insert stars into bow.

BANNER
From **A FESTIVE 4TH OF JULY** Ensemble *p. 222*

Designer: *Courtesy of Canvas Corp.*
Ink all edges.

1. Adhere blank canvases to burlap rectangles.
2. Trim patterned paper into banner strips; adhere.
3. Trim denim with pinking shears and adhere; draw stitches with pen.
4. Draw stitches on pennants with pen.
5. Cut firecrackers, stars, and hat from patterned paper, following patterns found on CD.
   Note: Mat hat with chalkboard paper and adhere corrugated paper brim. Adhere to pennants and burlap stars.
6. Draw stitches and lines with pens. Adhere rickrack.
7. Make spirals from wire and adhere.
8. Print letters on cardstock to spell "Welcome." Cut out and adhere.
9. Punch stars from patterned paper and adhere; draw lines with pen.
10. Punch starbursts from patterned paper and adhere.
11. Trim sentiments from patterned paper into banners; adhere.
12. Trim denim strips. Thread through metal stars and tie on to pennants; tie on to star tips; and adhere in loops and laces behind blank canvases.
13. Trim patterned paper and adhere to clothespins.
14. Thread rope through loops and attach stars and pennants with clothespins.

INVITATION
From A QUAINT HALLOWEEN
Ensemble *p. 235*

Designer: *Michelle Keeth, courtesy of Canvas Corp.*

❶ Stamp Barbed Wire, bird, you're invited, and invitation on large canvas triangle.
❷ Write sentiment.
❸ Trim cardstock strips into triangle. Stitch to large canvas rectangle; ink edges.

SPIDER BANNER
From A QUAINT HALLOWEEN
Ensemble *p. 235*

Designer: *Michelle Keeth, courtesy of Canvas Corp.*

❶ Paint four small burlap circles. Cut 32 spider legs from chalk stock, following pattern found on CD. Adhere to painted circles. Punch 32 circles from cardstock; adhere one to each leg. Adhere hemp rope behind three spiders.

❷ Trim candy corn pieces from patterned paper, following pattern. Ink edges and adhere to burlap triangles. Adhere final spider.

❸ Punch 20 circles from cardstock for masks and place on two large burlap circles; paint. Remove small cardstock circles. Punch circles from cardstock; draw borders and ink edges. Punch small circles from chalk stock and adhere to larger circles; adhere to burlap. Trim mouth from cardstock, following pattern. Draw border and adhere. Trim 16 legs from patterned paper, following pattern. Trim cardstock rectangles and adhere; ink edges. Trim 16 shoes from chalk stock, following pattern. Draw border. Trim cardstock strips with decorative-edge scissors; adhere to shoes. Trim chalk stock strips; apply chalk and adhere to shoes. Adhere pearls. Adhere legs to body. Adhere hemp rope behind spiders.

❹ Attach all pieces to jute rope with clothespins.

WITCH

From **A QUAINT HALLOWEEN**
Ensemble *p. 235*

Designer: Michelle Keeth, courtesy of Canvas Corp.

WITCH HEAD

1. Spray burlap heart and circle with shimmer spray; let dry.
2. Punch circles from cardstock. Draw borders with pen. Adhere circles together and adhere to burlap heart.
3. Trim mouth from cardstock, following pattern found CD. Mat with cardstock, trim, and draw border. Ink edges. Trim teeth from cardstock, following pattern. Adhere to mouth and adhere to burlap.
4. Adhere painted circle into nose; adhere. Adhere cork circles.
5. Trim hair from patterned paper, following pattern; ink edges. Adhere face.
6. Trim hat from specialty paper, following pattern.
7. Ink edges of patterned paper strip, adhere to hat, and trim edges.
8. Trim cardstock strips; adhere.
9. Adhere burlap star. Apply chalk to chalk stock; adhere. Adhere chalk stock rectangle.
10. Adhere clip behind head.

WITCH BODY

1. Spray canvas with shimmer spray.
2. Trim rectangles from chalk stock; trim edges with decorative-edge scissors. Ink edges and adhere to canvas.
3. Cut velvet fabric to 10" x 36"; pleat and staple to body. Adhere ribbon; tie ribbon bow and adhere.
4. Write sentiment with chalk.
5. Clip to head.

WITCH ARMS

1. Trim two strips of patterned paper to 8½" x 2½" for forearms; ink edges.
2. Trim two strips of patterned paper to 12" x 2½" for upper arms; adhere ribbon strips to patterned paper rectangles and adhere to forearms. Adhere forearms to upper arms.
3. Punch circles from patterned paper; adhere. Adhere buttons with dimensional glaze.
4. Trim hands from cardboard and burlap, following pattern found on CD. Spray burlap hands with shimmer spray; let dry. Adhere burlap hands to cardboard hands. Trim fingernails from chalk stock; adhere. Draw lines with pen. Adhere hands to arms.
5. Adhere clothespin behind hand; clip chalk to clothespin.
6. Attach to body with push pins.

WITCH LEGS

1. Trim 12 strips of patterned paper to 1" x 6"; ink edges and adhere into t[ ] chains.
2. Trim boots from chalk stock, following pattern found on CD. Apply chalk.
3. Trim four chalk stock rectangles; appl[ ] chalk to two rectangles and adhere rectangles to boots.
4. Adhere ribbon strips. Tie ribbon bow and adhere.
5. Adhere chains to boots. Attach to bo[ ] with push pins.

COASTER from **FUN ON THE FARM** Birthday Ensemble *p. 14.*

Designer: *Chan Vuong*

PENDANT from GRANDMA'S 70TH BIRTHDAY Ensemble *p. 22.*

Designer: *Julia Stainton*

BARRETTE from SWEET GIRL BIRTHDAY Ensemble *p. 60.*

Designer: *Wendy Sue Anderson*

CUPCAKE BOX from CUTE CUPCAKE PARTY Ensemble *p. 46.*

Designer: *Lucy Abrams*

THANK YOU TAG & RING from SWEET GIRL BIRTHDAY Ensemble *p. 60.*

Designer: *Wendy Sue Anderson*

A TOAST
to the happy couple

COASTER from URBAN CHIC ENGAGEMENT Ensemble *p. 72.*

Designer: *Andrea Bowden, courtesy of Stampin' Up!*

Swiss Fondue

Designer: Jennifer Schaerer

ⓐ NAPKIN RING

1. Mat patterned paper strip with cardstock.
2. Trim cross from cardstock, adhere to cardstock square, and adhere to panel.
3. Adhere panel together to create ring.

ⓑ BREAD SKEWER

1. Circle-punch cardstock.
2. Trim cross from cardstock, adhere to cardstock square, and adhere to circle.
3. Adhere piece to skewer.

ⓒ BANNER

1. Trim pennant patterns found on CD from cardstock and patterned paper. *Note: Save patterned paper scraps for Bread Bowl.*
2. Adhere pennants together with cardstock strips.
3. Die-cut "Fondue" from cardstock twice. Adhere together and adhere to pennants with foam tape.
4. Accordion-fold cardstock strips, ink pleats, and adhere to create rosettes.
5. Repeat steps 1-2 from Bread Skewer. Circle-punch cardstock and adhere crosses. Adhere pieces to rosettes.
6. Clip pennants to rope with clothespins. Adhere rosettes.

ⓓ BREAD BOWL

1. Make bowl from cardstock, following pattern found on included CD.
2. Adhere patterned paper. *Note: Use patterned paper scraps from Banner.*
3. Adhere cardstock strip and square.
4. Repeat steps 1-2 from Bread Skewer. Circle-punch cardstock and adhere cross. Adhere piece to bowl.

This book includes a CD with supplemental content such as supply lists and patterns. If the CD is missing or damaged, content can also be found at *www.PaperCraftsMag.com/downloads*